4/6

D0708418

AN OPEN-AIR ANTHOLOGY

AN OPEN-AIR
ANTHOLOGY

Compiled by

MARJORY SWINTON

COLLINS
LONDON AND GLASGOW

MAYFLOWER BOOKLETS
General Editor : G. F. Maine

Open the door and the world is yours.

STEPHEN GRAHAM
Gentle Art of Tramping

Printed in Great Britain by
COLLINS CLEAR-TYPE PRESS

CONTENTS

PROLOGUE

THERE is sweet music here that softer falls
Than petals from blown roses on the grass,
Or night-dews on still waters between walls
Of shadowy granite, in a gleaming pass;
Music that gentlier on the spirit lies,
Than tir'd eyelids upon tir'd eyes;
Music that brings sweet sleep down from the
blissful skies.
Here are cool mosses deep,
And through the moss the ivies creep,
And in the stream the long-leaved flowers weep,
And from the craggy ledge the poppy hangs in
sleep.

ALFRED TENNYSON
from *The Lotus-Eaters*

SPRING

Spring goeth all in white
Crowned with milk-white may.

ROBERT BRIDGES

WINTER IS PAST

For, lo, the winter is past, the rain is over and gone; the flowers appear on the earth; the time of the singing of birds is come, and the voice of the turtle is heard in our land.

SONG OF SOLOMON

NOW THAT THE WINTER'S GONE

Now that the winter's gone, the earth hath lost
Her snow-white robes: and now no more the frost
Candies the grass, or casts an icy cream
Upon the silver lake or crystal stream:
But the warm sun thaws the benumbèd earth
And makes it tender: gives a sacred birth
To the dead swallow; wakes in hollow tree
The drowsy cuckoo and the humble-bee.
Now do a choir of chirping minstrels bring,
In triumph to the world, the youthful Spring;
The valleys, hills, and woods, in rich array,
Welcome the coming of the longed-for May.
Now all things smile.

THOMAS CAREW

SONG

THE year's at the spring
  And day's at the morn;
Morning's at seven;
The hill-side's dew pearled;
The lark's on the wing;
The snail's on the thorn:
God's in His heaven—
All's right with the world!

ROBERT BROWNING

RETURN OF SPRING

Now fades the last long streak of snow,
  Now burgeons every maze of quick
About the flowering squares, and thick
By ashen roots the violets blow.

Now rings the woodland loud and long,
  The distance takes a lovelier hue,
  And drown'd in yonder living blue
The lark becomes a sightless song.

Now dance the lights on lawn and lea,
  The flocks are whiter down the vale,
  And milkier every milky sail
On winding stream or distant sea ;

Where now the seamew pipes, or dives
  In yonder greening gleam, and fly
  The happy birds, that change their sky
To build and brood ; that live their lives.

From land to land ; and in my breast
Spring wakens too ; and my regret
Becomes an April violet,
And buds and blossoms like the rest.

ALFRED TENNYSON

AWAKENING

THE air was sharp-set; a delicate rime frosted roof and road; the sea lay hazy and still like a great pearl. Then as the sky stirred with flush upon flush of warm rosy light, it passed from misty pearl to opal with heart of flame, from opal to gleaming sapphire. The earth called, the fields called, the river called—that pied piper to whose music a man cannot stop his ears. . . . A great blackbird flew out with a loud " chook, chook," and the red of the haw on his yellow bill. A robin trilled from a low rose-bush; two wrens searched diligently on a fallen tree for breakfast, quite unconcerned when I rested a moment beside them; and a shrewmouse slipped across the road followed directly by its mate. March violets bloomed under the sheltered hedge with here and there a pale primrose; a frosted bramble spray still held its autumn tints clinging to the semblance of the past; and great branches of snowy black-thorn broke the barren hedgeway as if spring made a mock of winter's snows.

MICHAEL FAIRLESS
from *The Roadmender*

TO SPRING

O THOU with dewy locks, who lookest down
Thro' the clear windows of the morning, turn
Thine angel eyes upon our western isle,
Which in full choir hails thy approach, O Spring.

The hills tell each other, and the list'ning
Valleys hear; all our longing eyes are turn'd
Up to thy bright pavilions, issue forth,
And let thy holy feet visit our clime.

Come o'er the eastern hills and let our winds
Kiss thy perfumèd garments; let us taste
Thy morn and evening breath; scatter thy pearls
Upon our love-sick land that mourns for thee.

O deck her forth with thy fair fingers; pour
Thy soft kisses on her bosom; and put
Thy golden crown upon her languish'd head
Whose modest tresses were bound up for thee.

WILLIAM BLAKE

ON A BANK AS I SAT A-FISHING

A Description of the Spring

A ND now all nature seemed in love;
The lusty sap began to move;
New juice did stir th' embracing vines,
And birds had drawn their valentines:

The jealous trout that low did lie,
Rose at a well-dissembled fly:
There stood my friend with patient skill,
Attending of his trembling quill.
Already were the eaves possessed
With the swift pilgrims' daubèd nest:
The groves already did rejoice
In Philomel's triumphing voice.
    The showers were short, the weather mild,
The morning fresh, the evening smiled.
Joan takes her neat-rubbed pail, and now
She trips to milk the sand red cow;
Where, for some sturdy football swain,
Joan strokes a sillabub, or twain.
    The field and gardens were beset
With tulip, crocus, violet;
And now, 'though late, the modest rose
Did more than half a blush disclose.
Thus all looked gay, all full of cheer,
To welcome the new-liveried year!

SIR HENRY WOTTON

ORPHEUS

ORPHEUS with his lute made trees,
And the mountain tops that freeze,
  Bow themselves, when he did sing;
To his music plants and flowers
Ever sprung; as sun and showers
  There had made a lasting spring.

Every thing that heard him play,
Even the billows of the sea,
   Hung their heads and then lay by.
In sweet music is such art,
Killing care and grief of heart
   Fall asleep or hearing die.

WILLIAM SHAKESPEARE
from *King Henry VIII, Act 3, Sc. 1*

SPRING

Sound the flute!
   Now it's mute.
Birds delight
Day and Night;
Nightingale
In the dale,
Lark in Sky,
Merrily,
Merrily, Merrily, to welcome in the Year.

Little Boy
Full of joy,
Little Girl
Sweet and small,
Cock does crow,
So do you;
Merry voice,
Infant noise,
Merrily, Merrily, to welcome in the Year.

Little Lamb
Here I am,
Come and lick
My white neck,
Let me pull
Your soft wool,
Let me kiss
Your soft face;
Merrily, Merrily, we welcome in the Year.

WILLIAM BLAKE

MORNING GLORY

THE cock had crowed, and now the eastern sky,
Was kindling, not unseen, from humble copse
And open field, through which the pathway
    wound,
And homeward led my steps. Magnificent
The morning rose, in memorable pomp,
Glorious as e'er I had beheld—in front,
The sea lay laughing at a distance; near,
The solid mountains shone, bright as the clouds,
Grain-tinctured, drenched in empyrean light;
And in the meadows and the lower grounds
Was all the sweetness of a common dawn—
Dews, vapours, and the melody of birds,
And labourers going forth to till the fields.

WILLIAM WORDSWORTH
from *The Prelude*, Bk. 4

WOOD AND MEADOW

ONCE at the summit under the beeches, and there a comfortable seat may be found upon the moss. The wood stretches away beneath for more than a mile in breadth, and beyond it winds the narrow mere glittering in the rays of the early spring sunshine. The bloom is on the blackthorn, but not yet on the may; the hedges are but just awakening from their long winter sleep, and the trees have hardly put forth a sign. But the rooks are busily engaged in the trees of the park, and away yonder at the distant colony in the elms of the meadows.

RICHARD JEFFERIES
from *The Gamekeeper at Home*

HARK, HARK, THE LARK

HARK, hark! the lark at heaven's gate sings,
    And Phoebus 'gins arise,
His steeds to water at those springs,
    On chalic'd flow'rs that lies;
And winking Mary-buds begin
    To ope their golden eyes.
With everything that pretty bin,
    My lady sweet, arise;
        Arise, arise!

WILLIAM SHAKESPEARE
from *Cymbeline, Act 2, Sc. 3*

COME, WHILE IN FRESHNESS AND DEW IT LIES

COME, while in freshness and dew it lies,
 To the world that is under the free blue skies!
Leave ye man's home, and forget his care—
There breathes no sigh on the dayspring's air.

Come to the woods, in whose mossy dells
A light all made for the poet dwells—
A light, coloured softly by tender leaves,
Whence the primrose a mellower glow receives.

The stock-dove is there in the beechen tree,
And the lulling tone of the honey-bee ;
And the voice of cool waters 'midst feathery fern,
Shedding sweet sounds from some hidden urn.

There is life, there is youth, there is tameless mirth,
Where the streams, with the lilies they wear, have
        birth;
There is peace where the alders are whispering
        low:
Come from man's dwellings with all their woe!

Yes! we will come—we will leave behind
The homes and the sorrows of human kind.
It is well to rove where the river leads
Its bright blue vein along sunny meads:

It is well through the rich wild woods to go,
And to pierce the haunts of the fawn and doe;

And to hear the gushing of gentle springs,
When the heart has been fretted by worldly stings;

And to watch the colours that flit and pass,
With insect-wings, through the wavy grass;
And the silvery gleams o'er the ash-tree's bark,
Borne in with a breeze through the foliage dark.

Joyous and far shall our wanderings be,
As the flight of birds o'er the glittering sea:
To the woods, to the dingles where violets blow,
We will bear no memory of earthly woe.

FELICIA HEMANS
from *The World in the Open Air*

A SPRING SONG

SEE the yellow catkins cover
All the slender willows over;
And on mossy barks so green
Star-like primroses are seen;
And their clustering leaves below
White and purple violets grow.

Hark the little lambs are bleating,
And the cawing rooks are meeting
In the elms—a noisy crowd;
And all birds are singing loud,
There, the first white butterfly
In the sun goes flitting by!

MARY HOWITT

GARLAND OF SPRING

Daffodils
That come before the swallow dares, and take
The winds of March with beauty; violets, dim,
But sweeter than the lids of Juno's eyes
Or Cytherea's breath; pale primroses,
That die unmarried ere they can behold
Bright Phoebus in his strength.

WILLIAM SHAKESPEARE
from *The Winter's Tale*, *Act 4, Sc. 4*

WRITTEN IN MARCH

The Cock is crowing
    The stream is flowing,
The small birds twitter,
The lake doth glitter,
The green fields sleep in the sun;
    The oldest and youngest
    Are at work with the strongest;
    The cattle are grazing,
    Their heads never raising;
There are forty feeding like one!

    Like an army defeated
    The snow hath retreated,
    And now doth fare ill
    On the top of the bare hill;
The ploughboy is whooping—anon—anon:

There's joy in the mountains;
There's life in the fountains;
Small clouds are sailing,
Blue sky prevailing;
The rain is over and gone!

WILLIAM WORDSWORTH

KINGCUPS

WHEN Spring revives in Arun's veins,
    And she grows restless day by day
With rushing storms of silver rains
    And speedy tides a league away,
And smells beneath her waving trees
The salt adventure of the seas:

Between her level banks she brims,
    And all the meadows overwhelms
Till solid earth in ocean swims,
    And huddled cows beneath the elms
Keep to their trodden path of mud
And watch their pastures under flood.

But when my lovely country lies
    Drowned in high waters and sweet scents,
Above the floods the kingcups rise
    In golden isles and continents,
Like an imagined world that leaps
To sight on momentary deeps.

Then through those seas of blue and steel,
  Where grasses like Pacific weeds
Hide many an ancient hulk and keel
  Of ships unhistoried with their deeds,
And tiny flowers submerged lie plain
Like sunken wonders of the main:

A giant adventurer I wade
  To conquest of the golden lands
Knee-deep in ocean unafraid,
  Amassing treasure with my hands,
Watched by astonished red-eyed cows
Banished from worlds they used to browse.

Not Cortez had such wealth as mine
  When on the fabulous floods for miles
The kingcups make the daylight shine
  With golden continents and isles,
And Spring outpours through Arun's streams
Her deluge of remembered dreams.

ELEANOR FARJEON

TO THE CUCKOO

Hail, beauteous stranger of the grove!
  Thou messenger of Spring!
Now Heaven repairs thy rural seat,
  And woods thy welcome ring.

What time the daisy decks the green,
  Thy certain voice we hear:

Hast thou a star to guide thy path,
  Or mark the rolling year?

Delightful visitant! with thee
  I hail the time of flowers,
And hear the sound of music sweet
  From birds among the bowers.

The schoolboy, wand'ring through the wood
  To pull the primrose gay,
Starts, the new voice of Spring to hear,
  And imitates thy lay.

What time the pea puts on the bloom,
  Thou fli'st thy vocal vale,
An annual guest in other lands,
  Another Spring to hail.

Sweet bird! thy bower is ever green,
  Thy sky is ever clear;
Thou hast no sorrow in thy song,
  No Winter in thy year!

O could I fly, I'd fly with thee!
  We'd make, with joyful wing,
Our annual visit o'er the globe,
  Companions of the Spring.

MICHAEL BRUCE

PRIMROSES

PRIMROSES cluster
In woodland glades, lighting the tender green
Like glints of sunshine.
Or 'midst brown leaves of last year's hazel growth
Their pale blooms shelter.
Pressing soft blossoms to our faces
We breathe their sweet, fresh airs and graces.

ETHEL FOLL

THE SPRINGHEAD

IN the narrow valley, far below the frowning
ramparts of the ancient fort a beautiful spring
breaks forth. Three irregular circular green spots,
brighter in colour than the dry herbage around,
mark the outlets of the crevices in the earth
through which the clear water finds its way to the
surface. Three tiny threads of water, each accom-
panied by its riband of verdant grasses, meander
downwards some few yards, and then unite and
form a little stream. Then the water in its channel
first becomes visible, glistening in the sun; for
at the sources the aquatic grasses bend over,
growing thickly and hide it from view. But pressing these down, and parting them with the hand,
you may trace the exact place where it rises,
gently oozing forth without a sound.

RICHARD JEFFERIES
from *Wild Life in a Southern County*

THE THRUSH

IN the swamp in secluded recesses
A shy and hidden bird is warbling a song
Solitary the thrush
The hermit withdrawn to himself avoiding the
    settlements
Sings by himself a song.
Song of the bleeding throat
Death's outlet song of life—(for well dear brother
I know
If thou wast not gifted to sing, thou would'st
    surely die)
Sing on, there in the swamp!
O singer bashful and tender! I hear your notes—
    I hear your call.
I hear—I come presently—I understand you:
But a moment I linger, for the lustrous star has
    detained me
The star, my departing comrade, holds and detains
    me.
Sing on, sing on, you gray-brown bird
Sing from the swamps, the recesses, pour your
    chant from the bushes.
Limitless out of the dusk, out of the cedars and
    pines
Sing on, dearest brother—warble your reedy song
Loud human song, with voice of uttermost woe,
O liquid and free and tender!
O wild and loose to my soul—O wondrous singer!

You only I hear—yet the star holds me (but will
    soon depart)
Yet the lilac with mastering odour holds me.

WALT WHITMAN

THE THRUSH'S NEST

WITHIN a thick and spreading hawthorn bush,
    That overhung a molehill large and round,
I heard from morn to morn a merry thrush
    Sing hymns to sunrise, and I drank the sound
With joy; and often, an intruding guest,
    I watched her secret toil from day to day—
How true she warped the moss, to form a nest,
    And modelled it within with wood and clay;
And by-and-by, like heath-bells gilt with dew,
    There lay her shining eggs, as bright as flowers,
Ink-spotted over shells of greeny blue;
    And there I witnessed in the sunny hours,
A brood of Nature's minstrels chirp and fly,
Glad as the sunshine and the laughing sky.

JOHN CLARE

TO THE CUCKOO

O BLITHE new-comer! I have heard,
    I hear thee and rejoice:
O cuckoo! shall I call thee Bird,
Or but a wandering Voice?

While I am lying on the grass
Thy twofold shout I hear;

From hill to hill it seems to pass,
At once far off and near.

Though babbling only to the vale
Of sunshine and of flowers,
Thou bringest unto me a tale
Of visionary hours.

Thrice welcome, darling of the Spring!
Even yet thou art to me
No bird, but an invisible thing,
A voice, a mystery;

The same whom in my school-boy days
I listened to; that cry
Which made me look a thousand ways
In bush, and tree, and sky.

To seek thee did I often rove
Through woods and on the green;
And thou wert still a hope, a love;
Still longed for, never seen!

And I can listen to thee yet;
Can lie upon the plain
And listen, till I do beget
That golden time again.

O blessèd bird! the earth we pace
Again appears to be
An unsubstantial, fairy place,
That is fit home for thee!

WILLIAM WORDSWORTH

FLOWERS

I HAVE in my rambles come upon two wonderfully beautiful flower effects, one in a Roman road, unused probably since Roman times. . . . When cycling over the high down country near Dorchester, I caught sight of what looked to me like a broad band of snow lying across the green hills. Coming to it I found the old Roman road, which is there very distinct and has a closer turf and a brighter green than the downs it lies across, so thickly overgrown with daisies that the crowded flowers were actually touching and had obliterated the green colour of the ground under them. It was a wonderful sight, for all these millions of small blossoms occupied the road only, not a daisy being seen on the green down on either side, and the loveliness was of so rare a quality, so rich yet so delicate, a beauty almost supernatural, that I could not bear to walk or ride on it. It was like a road leading to some unearthly brighter place—some paradise of flowers.

W. H. HUDSON
from *The Book of a Naturalist*

TO DAFFODILS

FAIR daffodils, we weep to see
    You haste away so soon:
As yet the early-rising Sun
    Has not attained his noon.

Stay, stay,
Until the hasting day
    Has run
But to the evensong;
And, having prayed together, we
    Will go with you along.

We have short time to stay, as you,
    We have as short a Spring!
As quick a growth to meet decay
    As you, or any thing.
        We die,
As your hours do, and dry
        Away
    Like to the Summer's rain;
Or as the pearls of morning's dew
    Ne'er to be found again.

ROBERT HERRICK

DAFFODILS

THERE before me lay spring's pageant; green
pennons waving, dainty maids curtseying, and
a host of joyous yellow trumpeters proclaiming
" Victory " to an awakened earth. They range in
serried ranks right down to the river, so that a
man must walk warily to reach the water's edge
where they stand gazing down at themselves in
fairest semblance like their most tragic progenitor,

and, rising from the bright grass in their thousands, stretch away until they melt in a golden cloud at the far end of the misty mead.

MICHAEL FAIRLESS
from *The Roadmender*

LITTLE TROTTY WAGTAIL

LITTLE trotty wagtail, he went in the rain,
And twittering, tottering sideways he ne'er
    got straight again.
He stooped to get a worm, and looked up to get
    a fly.
And then he flew away ere his feathers they were
    dry.

Little trotty wagtail, he waddled in the mud,
And left his little footmarks, trample where he
    would.
He waddled in the water-pudge, and waggle went
    his tail,
And chirrup up his wings to dry upon the garden
    rail.

Little trotty wagtail, you nimble all about,
And in the dimpling water-pudge you waddle in
    and out;
Your home is high at hand, and in the warm
    pig-stye,
So, little Master Wagtail, I'll bid you a good-bye.

JOHN CLARE

THE GREEN LINNET

BENEATH these fruit-tree boughs that shed
Their snow-white blossoms on my head,
With brightest sunshine round me spread
   Of spring's unclouded weather,
In this sequestered nook how sweet
To sit upon my orchard-seat!
And birds and flowers once more to greet,
   My last year's friends together.

One have I marked, the happiest guest
In all this covert of the blest:
Hail to Thee, far above the rest
   In joy of voice and pinion!
Thou, Linnet! in thy green array,
Presiding Spirit here to-day,
Dost lead the revels of the May;
   And this is thy dominion.

While birds, and butterflies, and flowers,
Make all one band of paramours,
Thou, ranging up and down the bowers,
   Art sole in thy employment:
A Life, a Presence like the Air,
Scattering thy gladness without care,
Too blest with any one to pair;
   Thyself thy own enjoyment.

Amid yon tuft of hazel trees,
That twinkle to the gusty breeze,

Behold him perched in ecstasies,
   Yet seeming still to hover;
There! where the flutter of his wings
Upon his back and body flings
Shadows and sunny glimmerings,
   That cover him all over.

My dazzled sight he oft deceives,
A brother of the dancing leaves;
Then flits, and from the cottage eaves
   Pours forth his song in gushes;
As if by that exulting strain
He mocked and treated with disdain
The voiceless Form he chose to feign,
   While fluttering in the bushes.

WILLIAM WORDSWORTH

THE LAMB

Little Lamb, who made thee?
  Dost thou know who made thee?
Gave thee life and bid thee feed
By the stream and o'er the mead:
Gave thee clothing of delight,
Softest clothing, woolly, bright;
Gave thee such a tender voice
Making all the vales rejoice?
   Little Lamb, who made thee?
   Dost thou know who made thee?

Little Lamb, I'll tell thee,
Little Lamb, I'll tell thee:
He is callèd by thy name,
For he calls himself a Lamb.
He is meek and he is mild;
He became a little child.
I a child and thou a lamb,
We are callèd by his name.
Little Lamb, God bless thee.
Little Lamb, God bless thee.

WILLIAM BLAKE

VIOLETS

THEY were the white wild violets, the sweetest of all, gathered while the nightingale was singing his morning song in the April sunshine— a song the world never listens to, more delicious than his evening notes, for the sunlight helps him, and the blue of the heavens, the green leaf, and the soft wind—all the soul of spring.

White wild violets, a dewdrop as it were of flower, tender and delicate, growing under the great hawthorn hedge, by the mosses and among the dry brown leaves of last year, easily overlooked unless you know exactly where to go for them.

RICHARD JEFFERIES

APRIL

The spring comes slowly up this way.
Christabel

'TIS the noon of the spring-time, yet never a
bird
In the wind-shaken elm or the maple is heard;
For green meadow-grasses wide levels of snow,
And blowing of drifts where the crocus should
blow;
Where wind-flower and violet, amber and white,
On south-sloping brooksides should smile in the
light,
O'er the cold winter-beds of their late-waking
roots
The frosty flake eddies, the ice-crystal shoots;
And, longing for light, under wind-driven heaps,
Round the boles of the pine-wood the ground-
laurel creeps,
Unkissed of the sunshine, unbaptized of showers,
With buds scarcely swelled, which should burst
into flowers!
We wait for thy coming, sweet wind of the south!
For the touch of thy light wings, the kiss of thy
mouth;
For the yearly evangel thou bearest from God,
Resurrection and life to the graves of the sod!
Up our long river-valley, for days, have not ceased
The wail and the shriek of the bitter north-east,—
Raw and chill, as if winnowed through ices and
snow,

All the way from the land of the wild Esquimaux,—
Until all our dreams of the land of the blest,
Like that red hunter's, turn to the sunny south-
    west.
O soul of the spring-time, its light and its breath,
Bring warmth to this coldness, bring life to this
    death;
Renew the great miracle; let us behold
The stone from the mouth of the sepulchre rolled,
And Nature, like Lazarus, rise, as of old!
Let our faith, which in darkness and coldness has
    lain,
Revive with the warmth and the brightness again,
And in blooming of flower and budding of tree
The symbols and types of our destiny see;
The life of the spring-time, the life of the whole,
And, as sun to the sleeping earth, love to the soul!
                                    JOHN G. WHITTIER

PHASES OF COLOUR

IN the spring the mowing-grass rises thick, strong
and richly green, or hidden by the cloth-of-gold
thrown over it by the buttercups. (The farmer)
knows when it is ready for the scythe without
reference to the almanac, because of the brown
tint which spreads over it from the ripening seeds,
sometimes tinged with a dull red, when the stems
of the sorrel are plentiful. At first the aftermath
has a trace of yellow, as if it were fading; but a
shower falls, and fresh green blades shoot up. Or,
passing from the hollow meads up on the rising

slopes where the plough rules the earth, what so beautiful to watch as the wheat through its various phases of colour?

First green and succulent; then, presently, see a modest ear comes forth with promise of the future. By-and-by, when every stalk is tipped like a sceptre, the lower stalk leaves are still green, but the stems have a faint bluish tinge, and the ears are paling into yellow. Next the white pollen—the bloom—shows under the warm sunshine, and then the birds begin to grow busy among it. They perch on the stalk itself—it is at that time strong and stiff enough to uphold their weight, one on a stem—but not now for mischief. You may see the sparrow carry away with him caterpillars for his young upon the house-top hard by; later on, it is true, he will revel on the ripe grains.

Yesterday you came to the wheat, and found it pale like this (it seems but twenty-four hours ago —it is really only a little longer); to-day, when you look again, lo! there is a fleeting yellow already on the ears. They have so quickly caught the hue of the bright sunshine pouring on them. Yet another day or two, and the faint fleeting yellow has become fixed and certain, as the colours are deepened by the great artist. Only when the wind blows and the ears bend in those places where the breeze takes most, it looks paler because the under part of the ear is shown and part of the stalk. Finally comes that rich hue for which no exact similitude exists. In it there is somewhat of

the red of the orange, somewhat of the tint of
bronze, and somewhat of the hue of maize; but
these are poor words wherewith to render fixed a
colour that plays over the surface of this yellow
sea, for if you take one, two, or a dozen ears you
shall not find it, but must look abroad, and let
your gaze travel to and fro. Nor is every field
alike; here are acres and acres more yellow,
yonder a space whiter, beyond that a slope richly
ruddy, according to the kind of seed that was sown.

Out of the depths of what to it must seem an
impenetrable jungle, from visiting a flower hidden
below, a humble-bee climbs rapidly up a stalk a
yard or two away while you look, and mounting
to the top of the ear, as a post of vantage clear of
obstructions, sails away upon the wind.

RICHARD JEFFERIES
from *Wild Life in a Southern County*

FLOWERS AND TREES

Boon nature scattered, free and wild,
Each plant or flower, the mountain's child.
Here eglantine embalmed the air,
Hawthorn and hazel mingled there;
The primrose pale, and violet flower,
Found in each cliff a narrow bower;
Fox-glove and night-shade, side by side,
Emblems of punishment and pride,
Grouped their dark hues with every stain
The weather-beaten crags retain.

With boughs that quaked at every breath,
Grey birch and aspen wept beneath;
Aloft, the ash and warrior oak
Cast anchor in the rifted rock;
And, higher yet, the pine-tree hung
His shattered trunk, and frequent flung,
Where seemed the cliffs to meet on high,
His boughs athwart the narrowed sky.
Highest of all, where white peaks glanced,
Where glistening streamers waved and danced,
The wanderer's eye could barely view
The summer heaven's delicious blue;
So wondrous wild, the whole would seem
The scenery of a fairy dream.

SIR WALTER SCOTT
from The Lady of the Lake

AN APRIL DAY

WHEN the warm sun, that brings
    Seed-time and harvest, has returned again,
'Tis sweet to visit the still wood, where springs
        The first flower of the plain.

I love the season well,
When forest glades are teeming with bright forms,
Nor dark and many-folded clouds foretell
        The coming-on of storms.

From the earth's loosened mould
The sapling draws its sustenance and thrives;

Though stricken to the heart with winter's cold,
    The drooping tree revives.

    The softly-warbled song
Comes from the pleasant woods, and coloured
    wings
Glance quick in the bright sun, that moves along
    The forest openings.

    When the bright sunset fills
The silver woods with light, the green slope throws
Its shadows in the hollows of the hills,
    And wide the upland glows.

    And, when the eve is born,
In the blue lake the sky, o'er-reaching far,
Is hollowed out, and the moon dips her horn,
    And twinkles many a star.

    Inverted in the tide,
Stand the gray rocks, and trembling shadows
    throw;
And the fair trees look over, side by side,
    And see themselves below.

    Sweet April!—many a thought
Is wedded unto thee, as hearts are wed;
Nor shall they fail, till, to its autumn brought,
    Life's golden fruit is shed.

HENRY W. LONGFELLOW

ORCHARD AND RICKYARD

AMONG the flowers here are beautiful dark-petalled wallflowers, sweet-williams, sweet-briar and pansies. In spring the yellow crocus lifts its head from among the grass of the green in front of the house (as the snowdrops did also), and here and there a daffodil. These, I think, never look so lovely as when rising from the greensward; the daffodils grow, too, in the orchard. Woodbine is everywhere—climbing over the garden seat under the sycamore tree, whose leaves are spotted sometimes with tiny reddish dots, the honey-dew.

Just outside the rickyard, where the grass of the meadow has not been mown but fed by cattle, grow the tall buttercups, rising to the knee. The children use the long hollow stems as tubes wherewith to suck up the warm new milk through its crown of thick froth from the oaken milking-pail. There is a fable that the buttercups make the butter yellow when they come—but the cows never eat them, being so bitter; they eat all round close up to the very stems, but leave them standing scrupulously. The children, too, make similar pipes of straw to suck up the new cider fresh from the cider-mill, as it stands in the tubs directly after the grinding. Under the shady trees of the orchard the hare's parsley flourishes, and immediately without the orchard edge, on the " shore " of the ditch, grow thick bunches of the beautiful blue

crane's-bill, or wild geranium, which ought to be
a garden flower and not left to the chance mercy
of the scythe. There, too, the herb Robert hides,
and its foliage, turning colour, lies like crimson
lace on the bank.

RICHARD JEFFERIES
from *Wild Life in a Southern County*

SONG ON MAY MORNING

Now the bright morning star, Day's harbinger,
    Comes dancing from the east, and leads with
        her
The flowery May, who from her green lap throws
The yellow cowslip and the pale primrose.
    Hail, bounteous May, that does inspire
    Mirth, and youth, and warm desire!
    Woods and groves are of thy dressing;
    Hill and dale doth boast thy blessing,
    Thus we salute thee with our early song,
    And welcome thee, and wish thee long.

JOHN MILTON

SUMMER

Now simmer blinks on flowery braes,
And o'er the crystal streamlet plays.

ROBERT BURNS

FAIR SUMMER

AGAIN the summer comes, and all is fair;
   A sea of tender blue, the sky o'erhead
Stretches its peace; the roses white and red
Through the deep silence of the tranced air,
In a mute ecstasy of love declare
Their souls in perfume, while their leaves are fed
With dew and moonlight that falls softly, shed
Like slumber on pure eyelids unaware.

PHILIP BOURKE MARSTON

THE INCOMING OF SUMMER

THE meadow grasses were not yet tall enough
   to sigh at the wind's soft passing, but a red
admiral had been joying in the sunlight for many
days. Down by the streamlet the moor-hen had
woven her rushy nest, bending an arch of withered
sedges over her labour to hide the speckled eggs.
In the mud of the pebbled shadows her webbed
feet left a track as she sought for beetles. Small
spoors, the imprint of little claws, showed where
a vole had made a quick passage across a mud-
bank. In the turfy bank its retreats were tunnelled,
leading to a domed hollow lined with grasses—
here her young would shortly nestle. From the
stream and the shallow the rushes were rising,

green spearpoints scarce sturdy enough to conceal the nest of the wild duck. Now they were thin and over-sharpened, as though exhausted by the effort of straining upwards to the light to which the sacrificial flowers would be offered in June; then they would be " thick and sappy," annealed; in winter the cattle would tread their dried stems upon the beaten floors of the shippen.

Over pebbles, wine-stained, gray, rusted, and brown, the stream tumbled, around mossy boulders and under branches, swaying dreamily the drowned poa grasses. Brook-trout lurked for the gnats that sometimes brushed the surface with trailing legs. Where the wind was stayed by arch of hazel and willow the midges danced their nuptials, in ghosted assembly rising and falling. The time of the mayflies was not yet, their brief pageant would be heralded by the myriad trumpets of summer insects; summer was still shyly virginal. No sunbeam had yet touched the buttercup, un-blazoned was the shield of the meadow by *gules* of poppy, *azure* of cornflower, or *argent* of feverfew. Fragile were the greeneries of the hedge above the brooklet, sweet the primroses under the stubbed roots of the ash-trees. Loveliest is the year when " sumer is icumen in," when the willow wren, slim as he perches on an amber wand, sings all the love in his heart.

HENRY WILLIAMSON
from *The Lone Swallows*

CUCKOO SONG

SUMMER is a-coming in,
    Sing a loud " cuckoo! "
The seed grows, the mead blows,
    The wood springs anew.
        Sing, cuckoo!

For her calf lows the cow;
    For her lamb bleats the ewe;
The bull rouses, the buck browses,
    Merrily sing, cuckoo!

Cuckoo, cuckoo, O, sing you well, cuckoo:
    Nor let your song be through:
Sing, cuckoo, now, sing cuckoo;
    Sing cuckoo, sing cuckoo, now!

ANON.

SUMMER SUNRISE

THE grey dawn awoke and stole with trailing robes across earth's floor. At her footsteps the birds roused from sleep and cried a greeting; the sky flushed and paled conscious of coming splendour; and overhead a file of swans passed with broad strong flight to the reeded waters of the sequestered pool.

Another hour of silence while the light throbbed

and flamed in the east; then the larks rose harmonious from a neighbouring field, the rabbits scurried with ears alert to their morning meal, the day had begun.

MICHAEL FAIRLESS
from *The Roadmender*

SUNRISE ON THE HILLS

I STOOD upon the hills, when heaven's wide arch
Was glorious with the sun's returning march,
And woods were brightened, and soft gales
Went forth to kiss the sun-clad vales.
The clouds were far beneath me; bathed in light,
They gathered midway round the wooded height,
And, in their fading glory, shone
Like hosts in battle overthrown,
As many a pinnacle, with shifting glance,
Through the gray mist thrust up its shattered lance,
And rocking on the cliff was left
The dark pine blasted, bare, and cleft.
The veil of cloud was lifted, and below
Glowed the rich valley, and the river's flow
Was darkened by the forest's shade,
Or glistened in the white cascade;
Where upward, in the mellow blush of day,
The noisy bittern wheeled his spiral way.

I heard the distant waters dash,
I saw the current whirl and flash,
And richly, by the blue lake's silver beach,

The woods were bending with a silent reach.
Then o'er the vale, with gentle swell,
The music of the village bell
Came sweetly to the echo-giving hills;
And the wild horn, whose voice the woodland fills,
Was ringing to the merry shout
That faint and far the glen sent out,
Where, answering to the sudden shot, thin smoke,
Through thick-leaved branches, from the dingle
    broke.
  If thou art worn and hard beset
With sorrows, that thou wouldst forget,
If thou wouldst read a lesson, that will keep
Thy heart from fainting and thy soul from sleep,
Go to the woods and hills! No tears
Dim the sweet look that Nature wears.

                        HENRY W. LONGFELLOW

DAWN ON LAKE KATRINE

THE summer dawn's reflected hue
  To purple changed Loch Katrine's blue;
Mildly and soft the western breeze
Just kissed the lake, just stirred the trees,
And the pleased lake, like maiden coy,
Trembled but dimpled not for joy;
The mountain-shadows on her breast
Were neither broken nor at rest;
In bright uncertainty they lie,
Like furtive joys to Fancy's eye.
The water-lily to the light

Her chalice reared of silver bright;
The doe awoke, and to the lawn,
Begemmed with dew-drops, led her fawn;
The grey mist left the mountain side,
The torrent showed its glistening pride;
Invisible in flecked sky,
The lark sent down her revelry;
The blackbird and the speckled thrush
Good-morrow gave from brake and bush;
In answer cooed the cushat dove
Her notes of peace, and rest and love.

SIR WALTER SCOTT
from *The Lady of the Lake*

THE MORNING SEA

CRADLED in sapphire mist, Morn's sunlit Deep
Wakes the whole world with laughter, dark-
ness past,
And with immeasurable music cast
Shoreward, 'mid sighs of strange relationship,
Earth's wandering mystic kinsman loves to keep
Her ear attent with mystery to the last,—
Whilst, like sea-butterflies with wings shut fast,
White ships walk summer seas in stately sleep.

Here fondling mother-like the pink-lipped shell,
That pearly grot or bubbling fountain paves,
Rocking the cradle of the asphodel,—
Yet all the while thou'rt thundering evermore,
With multitudinous hosts of armèd waves,
Loud at the gates of Thule's utmost shore!

CHARLES A. FOX

THE RAINBOW

AND the rainbow lives in the curve of the sand;
   Hither, come hither, and see;
And the rainbow hangs on the poising wave,
And sweet is the colour of cove and wave.

ALFRED TENNYSON

THE MELODIES OF MORN

BUT who the melodies of morn can tell?
   The wild brook babbling down the mountain
      side;
The lowing herd; the sheepfold's simple bell;
The pipe of early shepherd dim descried
In the lone valley; echoing far and wide
The clamorous horn along the cliffs above;
The hollow murmur of the ocean-tide;
The hum of bees, the linnet's lay of love,
And the full choir that wakes the universal grove.

The cottage-curs at early pilgrim bark;
Crowned with her pail the tripping milkmaid
      sings;
The whistling ploughman stalks afield; and,
      hark!
Down the rough slope the ponderous waggon
      rings;
Through rustling corn the hare astonished
      springs;

Slow tolls the village-clock the drowsy hour;
The partridge bursts away on whirring wings;
Deep mourns the turtle in sequestered bower.
And shrill lark carols clear from her aerial tower.

O Nature, how in every charm supreme!
Whose votaries feast on raptures ever new!
O for the voice and fire of seraphim,
To sing thy glories with devotion due!
Blest be the day I 'scaped the wrangling crew,
From Pyrrho's maze, and Epicurus' sty;
And held high converse with the godlike few,
Who to th' enraptured heart, and ear, and eye,
Teach beauty, virtue, truth, and love, and melody.

JAMES BEATTIE
from *The Minstrel*

PAGEANT OF SUMMER

GREEN rushes, long and thick, standing up
above the edge of the ditch, told the time of
the year as distinctly as the shadow on the dial
the hour of the day. Green and thick and sappy
to the touch, they felt like summer, soft and
elastic, as if full of life, mere rushes though they
were. On the fingers they left a green scent;
rushes have a separate scent of green; so, too,
have ferns, very different to that of grass or leaves.
Rising from brown sheaths, the tall stems enlarged
a little in the middle, like classical columns, and
heavy with their sap and freshness, leaned against

the hawthorn sprays. From the earth they had drawn its moisture, and made the ditch dry; some of the sweetness of the air had entered into their fibres, and the rushes—the common rushes—were full of beautiful summer.

RICHARD JEFFERIES
from *The Life of the Fields*

SUMMER DAWN

PRAY but one prayer for me 'twixt thy closed
    lips,
  Think but one thought of me up in the stars.
The summer night waneth, the morning light slips,
    Faint and grey 'twixt the leaves of the aspen,
      betwixt the cloud-bars,
That are patiently waiting there for the dawn:
  Patient and colourless, though Heaven's gold
Waits to float through them along with the sun.
Far out in the meadows, above the young corn,
  The heavy elms wait, and restless and cold
The uneasy wind rises; the roses are dun;
Through the long twilight they pray for the dawn,
Round the lone house in the midst of the corn.
  Speak but one word to me over the corn,
    Over the tender, bowed locks of the corn.

WILLIAM MORRIS

TO A SKYLARK

Hail to thee, blithe Spirit!
   Bird thou never wert,
That from heaven, or near it
   Pourest thy full heart
In profuse strains of unpremeditated art.

Higher still and higher
   From the earth thou springest
Like a cloud of fire;
   The blue deep thou wingest,
And singing still dost soar, and soaring ever singest.

In the golden lightning
   Of the sunken sun
O'er which clouds are bright'ning,
   Thou dost float and run,
Like an unbodied joy whose race is just begun.

The pale purple even
   Melts around thy flight;
Like a star of heaven
   In the broad daylight
Thou art unseen, but yet I hear thy shrill delight:

Keen as are the arrows
   Of that silver sphere,
Whose intense lamp narrows
   In the white dawn clear
Until we hardly see—we feel that it is there.

All the earth and air
　　With thy voice is loud,
As, when night is bare,
　　From one lonely cloud
The moon rains out her beams, and heaven is
　　overflowed.

What thou art we know not;
　　What is most like thee?
From rainbow clouds there flow not
　　Drops so bright to see
As from thy presence showers a rain of melody.

Like a poet hidden
　　In the light of thought,
Singing hymns unbidden,
　　Till the world is wrought
To sympathy with hopes and fears it heeded not:

Like a high-born maiden
　　In a palace tower,
Soothing her love-laden
　　Soul in secret hour
With music sweet as love, which overflows her
　　bower:

Like a glow-worm golden
　　In a dell of dew,
Scattering unbeholden
　　Its aërial hue
Among the flowers and grass, which screens it
　　from the view:

Like a rose embowered
  In its own green leaves,
By warm winds deflowered,
  Till the scent it gives
Makes faint with too much sweet these heavy-
    wingèd thieves.

Sound of vernal showers
  On the twinkling grass,
Rain-awakened flowers,
  All that ever was
Joyous, and clear, and fresh, thy music doth
    surpass.

Teach us, sprite or bird,
  What sweet thoughts are thine:
I have never heard
  Praise of love or wine
That panted forth a flood of rapture so divine.

Chorus hymeneal
  Or triumphal chaunt
Matched with thine, would be all
  But an empty vaunt—
A thing wherein we feel there is some hidden want.

What objects are the fountains
  Of thy happy strain?
What fields, or waves, or mountains?
  What shapes of sky or plain?
What love of thine own kind? what ignorance of
    pain?

With thy clear keen joyance
    Languor cannot be:
Shadow of annoyance
    Never came near thee:
Thou lovest, but ne'er knew love's sad satiety.

Waking or asleep,
    Thou of death must deem
Things more true and deep
    Than we mortals dream,
Or how could thy notes flow in such a crystal
    stream?

We look before and after,
    And pine for what is not:
Our sincerest laughter
    With some pain is fraught;
Our sweetest songs are those that tell of saddest
    thought.

Yet if we could scorn
    Hate, and pride, and fear;
If we were things born
    Not to shed a tear,
I know not how thy joy we ever should come near.

Better than all measures
    Of delightful sound,
Better than all treasures
    That in books are found,
Thy skill to poet were, thou scorner of the ground!

Teach me half the gladness
      That thy brain must know,
Such harmonious madness
      From my lips would flow
The world should listen then, as I am listening
      now!

PERCY B. SHELLEY

THE SUNBEAM

THOU art no lingerer in monarch's hall—
   A joy thou art, and a wealth to all!
A bearer of hope unto land and sea—
Sunbeam! what gift hath the world like thee?

Thou art walking the billows, and ocean smiles;
Thou hast touched with glory his thousand isles;
Thou hast lit up the ships and the feathery foam,
And gladdened the sailor like words from home.

To the solemn depths of the forest-shades,
Thou art streaming on through their green arcades;
And the quivering leaves that have caught thy
      glow
Like fire-flies glance to the pools below.

I looked on the mountains—a vapour lay
Folding their heights in its dark array;
Thou breakest forth, and the mist became
A crown and a mantle of living flame.

I looked on the peasant's lowly cot—
Something of sadness had wrapt the spot;
But a gleam of *thee* on its lattice fell,
And it laughed into beauty at that bright spell.

To the earth's wild places a guest thou art,
Flushing the waste like the rose's heart;
And thou scornest not from thy pomp to shed
A tender smile on the ruin's head.

Thou takest through the dim church-aisle thy way,
And its pillars from twilight flash forth to day,
And its high, pale tombs, with their trophies old,
Are bathed in a flood as of molten gold.

And thou turnest not from the humblest grave,
Where a flower to the sighing winds may wave;
Thou scatterest its gloom like the dreams of rest,
Thou sleepest in love on its grassy breast.

Sunbeam of summer! oh, what is like thee?
Hope of the wilderness, joy of the sea!—
One thing is like thee to mortals given,
The faith touching all things with hues of heaven!

FELICIA HEMANS

SWEET JARGONING

SOMETIMES a-dropping from the sky,
I heard the skylark sing;
Sometimes all little birds that are

How they seemed to fill the sea and air
With their sweet jargoning.

And now 'twas like an instrument,
Now like a lonely flute;
And now it is an angel's song
That makes the heavens grow mute.

SAMUEL T. COLERIDGE
from *The Ancient Mariner*

THERE WAS A MEADOW

THERE was a meadow level almost: you traced
The river wound about it as a waist.
Beyond, the banks were steep; a brush of trees
Rounded it, thinning skywards by degrees,
With parallel shafts,—as upward-parted ashes,—
Their highest sprays were drawn as fine as lashes,
With centres duly touch'd and nestlike spots,—
And oaks,—but these were leaved in sharper knots.
Great butter-burr leaves floor'd the slope corpse
    ground
Beyond the river, all the meadow's round,
And each a dinted circle. The grass was red
And long, the trees were colour'd, but the o'er-
    head,
Milky and dark, with an attuning stress
Controll'd them to a grey-green temperateness,
Making the shadow sweeter.

GERARD MANLEY HOPKINS
from *Richard*

TO A SKYLARK

ETHEREAL minstrel! pilgrim of the sky!
Dost thou despise the earth where cares
    abound?
Or, while the wings aspire, are heart and eye
Both with thy nest upon the dewy ground?
Thy nest which thou canst drop into at will,
Those quivering wings composed, that music still!
Leave to the nightingale her shady wood;
A privacy of glorious light is thine;
Whence thou dost pour upon the world a flood
Of harmony, with instinct more divine;
Type of the wise who soar, but never roam;
True to the kindred points of Heaven and home!

WILLIAM WORDSWORTH

MAY

MAY! queen of blossoms,
    And fulfilling flowers,
With what pretty music
    Shall we charm the hours?
Wilt thou have pipe and reed,
Blown in the open mead?
Or to the lute give heed
    In the green bowers?

Thou hast no need of us,
    Or pipe or wire,

Thou hast the golden bee
   Ripened with fire;
And many thousand more
Songsters, that thee adore,
Filling earth's grassy floor
   With new desire.

Thou hast thy mighty herds,
   Tame, and free livers;
Doubt not, thy music too
   In the deep rivers;
And the whole plumy flight,
Warbling the day and night:
Up at the gates of light,
   See, the lark quivers!

When with the jacinth
   Coy fountains are tressed;
And for the mournful bird
   Green woods are dressed,
That did for Tereus pine;
Then shall our songs be thine,
To whom our hearts incline:
   MAY, be thou blessed.

LORD THURLOW

WILD FLOWERS

I DO not want change; I want the same old and
loved things, the same wild flowers, the same
trees and soft ash-green; the turtle doves, the

blackbirds, the coloured yellow hammer, sing, sing, singing so long as there is light to cast a shadow on the dial, for such is the measure of his song, and I want them in the same place. Let me find them morning after morning, the starry-white petals radiating, striving upwards to their ideal. . . . Let me hear the humble bees, and stay to look down on the rich dandelion disk. Let me see the very thistles opening their great crowns. I should miss the thistles; the reed grasses hiding the moor-hen; the bryony brine, at first crudely ambitious and lifted by force of youthful sap straight above the hedgerow to sink of its own weight presently and progress with crafty tendrils; swifts shot through the air with outstretched wings like crescent-headed, shaftless arrows darted from the clouds; the chaffinch, all the living staircase of the Spring, step by step, upwards to the great gallery of the summer—let me watch the same succession year by year.

RICHARD JEFFERIES
from *The Open Air*

ODE TO LEVEN WATER

ON Leven's banks, while free to rove,
And tune the rural pipe to Love,
I envied not the happiest swain
That ever trod th' Arcadian plain.
Pure stream! in whose transparent wave
My youthful limbs I wont to lave;

No torrents stain thy limpid source;
No rocks impede thy dimpling course,
That sweetly warbles o'er its bed,
With white, round, polished pebbles spread;
While, lightly poised, the scaly brood
In myriads cleave thy crystal flood;
The springing trout in speckled pride;
The salmon, monarch of the tide;
The ruthless pike, intent on war;
The silver eel, the mottled par.
Devolving from thy parent lake,
A charming maze thy waters make,
By bowers of birch, and groves of pine,
And hedges flowered with eglantine.

    Still on thy banks so gaily green,
May numerous herds and flocks be seen,
And lasses chanting o'er the pail,
And shepherds piping in the dale,
And ancient faith that knows no guile,
And industry embrowned with toil;
And hearts resolved, and hands prepared,
The blessings they enjoy to guard!

TOBIAS GEORGE SMOLLETT

JUNE

AND what is so rare as a day in June?
    Then, if ever, come perfect days;
Then Heaven tries earth if it be in tune,
    And over it softly her warm ear lays:
Whether we look, or whether we listen,

We hear life murmur, or see it glisten;
Every clod feels a stir of might,
    An instinct within it that reaches and towers,
And, groping blindly above it for light,
    Climbs to a soul in grass and flowers;
The flush of life may well be seen
    Thrilling back over hills and valleys;
The cowslip startles in meadows green,
    The buttercup catches the sun in its chalice,
And there's never a leaf nor a blade too mean
    To be some happy creature's palace;
The little bird sits at his door in the sun
    Atilt like a blossom among the leaves,
And let his illumined being o'errun
    With the deluge of summer it receives;
His mate feels the eggs beneath her wings,
And the heart in her dumb breast flutters and
        sings;
He sings to the wide world, and she to her nest,—
In the nice ear of Nature which song is the best?

Now is the high-tide of the year,
    And whatever of life hath ebbed away
Comes flooding back with a ripply cheer,
    Into every bare inlet and creek and bay;
Now the heart is so full that a drop overfills it,
We are happy now because God wills it;
No matter how barren the past may have been,
'Tis enough for us now that the leaves are green;
We sit in the warm shade and feel right well
How the sap creeps up and the blossoms swell;

We may shut our eyes, but we cannot help knowing
That skies are clear and grass is growing;
The breeze comes whispering in our ear,
That dandelions are blossoming near,
    That maize has sprouted, that streams are
       flowing,
That the river is bluer than the sky,
That the robin is plastering his house hard by;
And if the breeze keeps the good news back,
For other couriers we shall not lack;
    We could guess it all by yon heifer's lowing,—
And hark! how clear bold chanticleer,
Warmed with the new wine of the year,
    Tells all in his lusty crowing!

JAMES R. LOWELL
from *The Vision of Sir Launfal*

THE SONG OF THE LARK

PHILOMEL will deign a song,
  In her sweetest, saddest plight,
Smoothing the rugged brow of night,
While Cynthia checks her dragon yoke,
Gently o'er th' accustomed oak;
Sweet bird that shunn'st the noise of folly,
Most musical, most melancholy!
Thee, chantress, oft the woods among,
I woo to hear thy evensong;
And missing thee, I walk unseen
On the dry smooth-shaven green,
To behold the wandering moon,

Riding near her highest noon,
Like one that had been led astray
Through the Heavens' wide pathless way;
And oft, as if her head she bowed,
Stooping through a fleecy cloud.
Oft on a plat of rising ground,
I hear the far-off curfew sound,
Over some wide-watered shore,
Swinging slow with sullen roar.

JOHN MILTON
from *Il Penseroso*

THE HUMBLE-BEE

BURLY, dozing humble-bee,
Where thou art is clime for me.
Let them sail for Porto Rique,
Far-off heats through seas to seek;
I will follow thee alone,
Thou animated torrid-zone!
Zigzag steerer, desert cheerer,
Let me chase thy waving lines;
Keep me nearer, me thy hearer,
Singing over shrubs and vines.

Insect lover of the sun,
Joy of thy dominion!
Sailor of the atmosphere;
Swimmer through the waves of air;
Voyager of light and noon;
Epicurean of June;

Wait, I prithee, till I come
Within earshot of thy hum,—
All without is martyrdom.

When the south wind, in May days,
With a net of shining haze
Silvers the horizon wall,
And, with softness touching all,
Tints the human countenance
With a colour of romance,
And, infusing subtle heats,
Turns the sod to violets,
Thou, in sunny solitudes,
Rover of the underwoods,
The green silence dost displace
With thy mellow, breezy bass.

Hot midsummer's petted crone,
Sweet to me thy drowsy tone
Tells of countless sunny hours,
Long days, and solid banks of flowers;
Of gulfs of sweetness without bound
In Indian wildernesses found;
Of Syrian peace, immortal leisure,
Firmest cheer, and bird-like pleasure.

Aught unsavoury or unclean
Hath my insect never seen;
But violets and bilberry bells,
Maple-sap, and daffodels,
Grass with green flag half-mast high,

Succory to match the sky,
Columbine with horn of honey,
Scented fern, and agrimony,
Clover, catchfly, adder's-tongue,
And brier-roses, dwelt among;
All beside was unknown waste,
All was picture as he passed.

Wiser far than human seer,
Yellow-breeched philosopher!
Seeing only what is fair,
Sipping only what is sweet,
Thou dost mock at fate and care,
Leave the chaff, and take the wheat.
When the fierce northwestern blast
Cools sea and land so far and fast,
Thou already slumberest deep;
Woe and want thou canst outsleep;
Want and woe, which torture us,
Thy sleep makes ridiculous.

RALPH W. EMERSON

CONTINUAL SLIGHT VARIETY

THE sea, alone of natural things, obeys Aristotle's law in art, that for perfect pleasure there must be continual slight variety. It has the monotony of great art, and its continual slight variety. Everything else in nature wearies one by its stillness or its restlessness; by a limit which suggests constraint or by an open bareness which is but lawless and uncultured. But here the eye travels easily on to heaven; there is only that diamond barrier of sky between it and the end of the world. And the world itself seems no longer to have a limit; and, by these gentle degrees, infinity itself loses its horror.

ARTHUR SYMONS
from Cornish Sketches

SUDDEN SHOWER

BLACK grows the sudden sky, betokening rain,
    And humming hive-bees homeward hurry by:
They feel the change; so let us shun the grain,
    And take the broad road while our feet are dry.
Aye there, some drops fell moistening on my face,
    And pattering on my hat—'tis coming nigh!—
Let's look about, and find a sheltering place.
    The little things around us fear the sky,
And hasten through the grass to shun the shower.
    Here stoops an ash-tree—hark! the wind gets high,
But never mind; this ivy for an hour,
    Rain as it may, will keep us drily here:
That little wren knows well his sheltering bower,
    Nor leaves his covert, though we come so near.

JOHN CLARE

THE SEA FLOWER

A<small>ND</small> as the august blossom of the dawn
 Burst, and the full sun scarce from sea with-
drawn
Seemed on the fiery water a flower afloat.

A. C. SWINBURNE

THE MYSTERY OF SPACE

A<small>LL</small> night by the shore.
 The obscure water, the long white lines of
advancing foam—the rustle and thud, the panting
sea breaths, the sea-smell—
 The great slow air moving from the distant
horizon—the immense mystery of space, and the
soft canopy of the clouds.

EDWARD CARPENTER

ODE TO A NIGHTINGALE

My heart aches, and a drowsy numbness pains
 My sense, as though of hemlock I had drunk,
Or emptied some dull opiate to the drains
 One minute past, and Lethe-wards had sunk:
'Tis not through envy of thy happy lot,
 But being too happy in thy happiness,—
  That thou, light-wingèd Dryad of the trees,
   In some melodious plot
Of beechen green, and shadows numberless,
 Singest of summer in full-throated ease.

O for a draught of vintage, that hath been
    Cooled a long age in the deep-delvèd earth,
Tasting of Flora and the country green,
    Dance, and Provençal song, and sun-burnt
        mirth!
O for a beaker full of the warm South,
        Full of the true, the blushful Hippocrene,
            With beaded bubbles winking at the brim,
                And purple-stainèd mouth;
        That I might drink, and leave the world
            unseen,
            And with thee fade away into the forest dim:

Fade far away, dissolve, and quite forget
    What thou among the leaves hast never known,
The weariness, the fever, and the fret
    Here, where men sit and hear each other groan;
Where palsy shakes a few, sad, last grey hairs,
    Where youth grows pale, and spectre-thin, and
        dies;
        Where but to think is to be full of sorrow
            And leaden-eyed despairs;
    Where beauty cannot keep her lustrous eyes,
        Or new love pine at them beyond to-morrow.

Away! away! for I will fly to thee,
    Not charioted by Bacchus and his pards,
But on the viewless wings of Poesy,
    Though the dull brain perplexes and retards:
Already with thee! tender is the night,
    And haply the Queen-Moon is on her throne,

Clustered around by all her starry fays;
But here there is no light,
Save what from heaven is with the breezes blown
Through verdurous glooms and winding
mossy ways.

I cannot see what flowers are at my feet,
Nor what soft incense hangs upon the boughs,
But, in embalmèd darkness, guess each sweet
Wherewith the seasonable month endows
The grass, the thicket, and the fruit-tree wild;
White hawthorn, and the pastoral eglantine;
Fast-fading violets covered up in leaves;
And mid-May's eldest child,
The coming musk-rose, full of dewy wine,
The murmurous haunt of flies on summer eves.

Darkling I listen; and for many a time
I have been half in love with easeful Death,
Called him soft names in many a musèd rhyme,
To take into the air my quiet breath;
Now more than ever seems it rich to die,
To cease upon the midnight with no pain,
While thou art pouring forth thy soul abroad
In such an ecstasy!
Still wouldst thou sing, and I have ears in vain—
To thy high requiem become a sod.

Thou wast not born for death, immortal Bird!
No hungry generations tread thee down;
The voice I hear this passing night was heard

In ancient days by emperor and clown:
Perhaps the self-same song that found a path
    Through the sad heart of Ruth, when, sick for
        home,
        She stood in tears amid the alien corn;
            The same that oft-times hath
    Charmed magic casements, opening on the foam
        Of perilous seas, in faery lands forlorn.

Forlorn! the very word is like a bell
    To toll me back from thee to my sole self.
Adieu! the fancy cannot cheat so well
    As she is famed to do, deceiving elf.
Adieu! adieu! thy plaintive anthem fades
    Past the near meadows, over the still stream,
        Up the hill-side; and now 'tis buried deep
            In the next valley-glades:
    Was it a vision, or a waking dream?
        Fled is that music:—do I wake or sleep?

JOHN KEATS

THE MUSIC OF EARTH

THE very birds of the air are both so many and
so pleasant to mankind, that I must not let
them pass without some observations.

As first the lark, when she means to rejoice,
to cheer herself and those that hear her; she then
quits the earth, and sings as she ascends higher
into the air, and having ended her heavenly
employment, grows then mute and sad, to think

she must descend to the dull earth, which she would not touch, but for necessity.

How do the blackbird, and thrassel, with their melodious voices bid welcome to the cheerful spring, as in their fixed months warble forth such ditties as no art or instrument can reach to!

Nay, the smaller birds also do the like in their particular seasons, as namely the leverock, the titlark, the little linnet, and the honest robin, that loves mankind both alive and dead.

But the nightingale, another of my airy creatures, breathes such sweet loud music out of her little instrumental throat that it might make mankind to think miracles are not ceased. He that at midnight, when the very labourer sleeps securely, should hear, as I have very often, the clear airs, the sweet descants, the natural rising and falling, the doubling and redoubling of her voice, might well be lifted above earth, and say, " Lord, what music hast Thou provided for the saints in heaven, when Thou affordest bad men such music on earth? "

IZAAK WALTON
from *The Compleat Angler*

PUCK'S SONG

Over hill, over dale,
    Thorough bush, thorough brier,
Over park, over pale,
    Thorough flood, thorough fire,

I do wander every where,
Swifter than the moon's sphere;
And I serve the Fairy Queen,
To dew her orbs upon the green.
The cowslips tall her pensioners be;
In their gold coats spots you see;
Those be rubies, fairy favours,
In those freckles live their savours:
I must go seek some dewdrops here,
And hang a pearl in every cowslip's ear.

WILLIAM SHAKESPEARE
from *A Midsummer Night's Dream, Act 2, Sc.1*

THE BEANFIELD

A BEANFIELD in blossom smells as sweet
As Araby, or groves of orange flowers;
Black-eyed and white, and feathered to one's feet,
How sweet they smell in morning's dewy hours.
When seething night is left upon the flowers,
Another morn's sun shines brightly o'er the field,
The bean bloom glitters in the gem of showers,
And sweet the fragrance which the union yields
To battered footpaths crossing o'er the fields.

JOHN CLARE

A DAY IN JUNE

IT was a bright and cheerful afternoon,
Towards the end of the sunny month of June,
When the north wind congregates in crowds
The floating mountains of the silver clouds
From the horizon—and the stainless sky
Opens beyond them like eternity.
All things rejoiced beneath the sun; the weeds,
The river, and the corn-fields, and the reeds;
The willow leaves that glanced in the light breeze,
And the firm foliage of the larger trees.

PERCY B. SHELLEY
from *Summer and Winter*

THE RIVER

PERHAPS the river is sweetest to look on in springtime or early summer. Seen from a distance the water seems at first sight, when the broad stream fills the vision as a whole, to flow with smooth, even current between meadow and cornfield. But coming to the brink, that silvery surface now appears exquisitely chased with ever-changing lines. The light airs, wandering to and fro where the high banks exclude the direct influence of the breeze, flutter the ripples hither and thither, so that instead of rolling on one lee shore, they meet and expend their little force upon each other. A continuous rising and falling, without a line of direction, thus breaks up the light, not with sparkle or glitter, but with endless silvery facets.

There is no pattern. The apparently intertangled tracing on a work of art presently resolves itself into a design, which once seen is always the same. These wavelets form no design; watch the sheeny maze as long as one will, the eye cannot get at the clue and so unwind the pattern.

RICHARD JEFFERIES
from *Nature near London*

THE RIVER GLIDETH

Thus the Mayne glideth
Where my Love abideth;
Sleep's no softer: it proceeds
On through lawns, on through meads,
On and on, whate'er befall,
Meandering and musical,
Though the niggard pasturage
Bears not on its shaven edge
Aught but weeds and waving grasses
To view the river as it passes,
Save here and there a scanty patch
Of primroses too faint to catch
A weary bee . . . And scarce it pushes
Its gentle way through straggling rushes
Where the glossy king-fisher
Flutters when noon-heats are near,
Glad the shelving banks to shun,
Red and steaming in the sun,

Where the shrew-mouse with pale throat
Burrows, and the speckled stoat;
Where the quick sandpipers flit
In and out the marl and wet
That seems to breed them, brown as they:
Naught disturbs its quiet way,
Save some lazy stork that springs,
Trailing it with legs and wings,
Whom the shy fox from the hill
Rouses, creep he ne'er so still.

ROBERT BROWNING
from *Paracelsus*

THE MAY AND THE ROSE

IT was between the may and the June roses.
The may bloom had fallen, and among the
hawthorn boughs were the little green bunches
that would feed the redwings in autumn. High
up the briars had climbed, straight and towering
while there was a thorn or an ash sapling, or a
yellowgreen willow, to uphold them, and then
curving over towards the meadow. The buds
were on them, but not yet open; it was between
the may and the rose.

RICHARD JEFFERIES
from *The Life of the Fields*

A THING OF BEAUTY

A THING of beauty is a joy for ever:
Its loveliness increases; it will never
Pass into nothingness; but still will keep
A bower quiet for us, and a sleep
Full of sweet dreams, and health, and quiet
   breathing.
Therefore, on every morrow, are we wreathing
A flowery band to bind us to the earth,
Spite of despondence, of the inhuman dearth
Of noble natures, of the gloomy days,
Of all the unhealthy and o'er-darkened ways
Made for our searching: yes, in spite of all,
Some shape of beauty moves away the pall
From our dark spirits. Such the sun, the moon,
Trees old and young, sprouting a shady boon
For simple sheep; and such are daffodils
With the green world they live in; and clear rills
That for themselves a cooling covert make
'Gainst the hot season; the mid-forest brake,
Rich with a sprinkling of fair musk-rose blooms.

JOHN KEATS
from *Endymion*

TO A WATERFOWL

WHITHER, 'midst falling dew,
While glow the heavens with the last steps of
   day,
Far, through their rosy depths, dost thou pursue
   Thy solitary way!

Vainly the fowler's eye
Might mark thy distant flight to do three wrong,
As, darkly painted on the crimson sky,
    Thy figure floats along.

Seek'st thou the plashy brink
Of weedy lake, or marge of river wide,
Or where the rocking billows rise and sink
    On the chafed ocean side?

There is a power whose care
Teaches thy way along that pathless coast,—
The desert and illimitable air,—
    Lone wandering, but not lost.

All day thy wings have fanned,
At that far height, the cold, thin atmosphere,
Yet stoop not, weary, to the welcome land,
    Though the dark night is near.

And soon that toil shall end;
Soon shalt thou find a summer home, and rest,
And scream among thy fellows; reeds shall bend,
    Soon, o'er thy sheltered nest.

Thou'rt gone, the abyss of heaven
Hath swallowed up thy form; yet, on my heart
Deeply hath sunk the lesson thou hast given,
    And shall not soon depart.

He who, from zone to zone,
Guides through the boundless sky thy certain
    flight,
In the long way that I must tread alone,
    Will lead my steps aright.

WILLIAM C. BRYANT

A BORDER BURN

OH, Tam! Gie me a Border burn
    That canna rin without a turn,
And wi' its bonnie babble fills
The glens among oor native hills.
How men that ance have ken'd aboot it
Can leeve their after-lives without it
I canna tell, for day and nicht
It comes unca'd for to my sicht.
I see't this moment, plain as day,
As it comes bickerin' ower the brae,
Atween the clumps o' purple heather
Glistenin' in the summer weather,
Syne drivin' in below the grun'
Where, hidden frae sicht and sun,
It gibbers like a deid man's ghost
That clamours for the licht it's lost,
Till oot again the loupin' limmer,
Comes dancin' doon through shine and shimmer
At heidlang pace, till wi' a jaw
It jumps the rocky waterfa',
And cuts sic cantrips in the air,
The picter-pentin' man's despair;

A row'ntree bus' oot ower the top o't,
A glassy pule—to kep the lap o't,
While on the brink the blue harebell
Keeks ower to see it's bonny sel'.
And sittin' chirpin' a' its lane
A water-waggy on a stane,
Ay, penter lad, thraw to the wund
Your canvas, this is holy grund;
Wi' a' its higher airt acheevin',
That picter's deid, and this is leevin'!

J. B. SELKIRK

THE FLY

LITTLE Fly,
Thy summer's play
My thoughtless hand
Has brushed away.

Am not I
A fly like thee?
Or art not thou
A man like me?

For I dance
And drink and sing,
Till some blind hand
Shall brush my wing.

If thought is life
And strength and breath,
And the want
Of thought is death,

Then am I
A happy fly
If I live
Or if I die.

WILLIAM BLAKE

THE MIGHTY OCEAN

IT keeps eternal whisperings around
Desolate shores, and with its mighty swell
Gluts twice ten thousand caverns.

JOHN KEATS

WATER-FOWL

MARK how the feathered tenants of the flood,
With grace of motion that might scarcely seem
Inferior to angelical, prolong
Their curious pastime! shaping in mid air
(And sometimes with ambitious wing that soars
High as the level of the mountain tops)
A circuit ampler than the lake beneath,
Their own domain;—but ever, while intent

On tracing and retracing that large round,
Their jubilant activity evolves
Hundreds of curves and circles, to and fro,
Upward and downward, progress intricate,
Yet unperplexed, as if one spirit swayed
Their indefatigable flight.—'Tis done—
Ten times, or more, I fancied it had ceased;
But lo! the vanished company again
Ascending;—they approach—I hear their wings
Faint, faint at first; and then an eager sound
Past in a moment—and as faint again!
They tempt the sun to sport amid their plumes;
They tempt the water, or the gleaming ice,
To show them a fair image;—'tis themselves,
Their own fair forms, upon the glimmering plain,
Painted more soft and fair as they descend
Almost to touch;—then up again aloft,
Up with a sally and a flash of speed,
As if they scorned both resting-place and rest!

WILLIAM WORDSWORTH

SILENCE

THE world so hushed!
The stilly murmur of the distant sea
Tells us of silence

SAMUEL T. COLERIDGE

WHITE BUTTERFLIES

THE lightest things are blind to their own powers;
   These butterflies, that flicker through the hours
Of summer, are the ghosts of last year's flowers.

Their green-white wings are scattered in the sun
Like petals drained of colour, idly spun
And twitched by the faint laughter from beneath,
From the usurpers, firm in stem and sheath
And in the neighbourhood of life, to grow
According to the season's rise and flow.

While the detached white phantoms overhead,
Free with the sightless freedom of the dead,
Haunt their lost world of yellow, gold, and red.

VERA N. WYLDE

LINGER AWHILE

LINGER awhile upon some bending planks
   That lean against a streamlet's rushy banks,
And watch intently Nature's gentle doings:
They will be found softer than ring-dove's cooings.
How silent comes the water round that bend;
Not the minutest whisper does it send
To the o'erhanging sallows: blades of grass
Slowly across the chequer'd shadows pass.
Why, you might read two sonnets, ere they reach
To where the hurrying freshnesses aye preach

A natural sermon o'er their pebbly beds;
Where swarms of minnows show their little heads,
Staying their wavy bodies 'gainst the streams,
To taste the luxury of sunny beams
Temper'd with coolness.

JOHN KEATS
from *I Stood Tiptoe upon a Little Hill*

TO MEADOWS

YE have been fresh and green,
  Ye have been filled with flowers.
And ye the walks have been
  Where maids have spent their hours.

You have beheld how they
  With wicker arks did come
To kiss and bear away
  The richer cowslips home.

You've heard them sweetly sing,
  And seen them in a round:
Each virgin like a spring,
  With honeysuckles crowned.

But now we see none here
  Whose silvery feet did tread
And with dishevelled hair
  Adorned this smoother mead.

Like unthrifts, having spent
    Your stock and needy grown,
You're left here to lament
    Your poor estates, alone.

ROBERT HERRICK

LOVELIEST VILLAGE

SWEET Auburn, loveliest village of the plain,
    Where health and plenty cheered the labouring
    swain,
Where smiling spring its earliest visit paid,
And parting summer's lingering blooms delayed.
Dear lovely bowers of innocence and ease,
Seats of my youth, when every sport could please,
How often have I loitered o'er thy green,
Where humble happiness endeared each scene!
How often have I paused on every charm,
The sheltered cot, the cultivated farm,
The never-failing brook, the busy mill,
The decent church that topped the neighbouring
    hill,
The hawthorn bush, with seats beneath the shade,
For talking age and whispering lovers made!
How often have I blessed the coming day,
When toil remitting lent its turn to play,
And all the village train, from labour free,
Led up their sports beneath the spreading tree,
While many a pastime circled in the shade,
The young contending as the old surveyed;

And many a gambol frolicked o'er the ground,
And sleights of art and feats of strength went
    round;
And still as each repeated pleasure tired,
Succeeding sports the mirthful band inspired:
The dancing pair that simply sought renown,
By holding out, to tire each other down.

OLIVER GOLDSMITH
from *The Deserted Village*

THE CLOUD

I BRING fresh showers for the thirsting flowers,
    From the seas and the streams;
I bear light shade for the leaves when laid
    In their noonday dreams.
From my wings are shaken the dews that waken
    The sweet buds every one,
When rocked to rest on their mother's breast,
    As she dances about the sun.
I wield the flail of the lashing hail,
    And whiten the green plains under,
And then again I dissolve it in rain,
    And laugh as I pass in thunder.
I sift the snow on the mountains below,
    And their great pines groan aghast;
And all the night 'tis my pillow white,
    While I sleep in the arms of the blast.
Sublime on the towers of my skiey bowers,
    Lightning, my pilot, sits;

In a cavern under is fettered the thunder,
    It struggles and howls at fits;
Over earth and ocean, with gentle motion,
    This pilot is guiding me,
Lured by the love of the genii that move
    In the depths of the purple sea;
Over the rills, and the crags, and the hills,
    Over the lakes and the plains,
Wherever he dream, under mountain or stream,
    The Spirit he loves remains;
And I all the while bask in Heaven's blue smile,
    Whilst he is dissolving in rains.

The sanguine Sunrise, with his meteor eyes,
    And burning plumes outspread,
Leaps on the back of my sailing rack,
    When the morning star shines dead;
As on the jag of a mountain crag,
    Which an earthquake rocks and swings,
An eagle alit one moment may sit
    In the light of its golden wings.
And when Sunset may breathe, from the lit sea beneath,
    Its ardours of rest and love,
And the crimson pall of eve may fall
    From the depth of Heaven above,
With wings folded I rest, on mine aery nest,
    As still as a brooding dove.

That orbèd maiden with white fire laden,
  Whom mortals call the Moon,
Glides glimmering o'er my fleece-like floor,
  By the midnight breezes strewn;
And wherever the beat of her unseen feet,
  Which only the angels hear,
May have broken the woof of my tent's thin roof,
  The stars peep behind her and peer;
And I laugh to see them whirl and flee,
  Like a swarm of golden bees,
When I widen the rent in my wind-built tent,
  Till the calm rivers, lakes, and seas,
Like strips of the sky fallen through me on high,
  Are each paved with the moon and these.

I bind the Sun's throne with a burning zone,
  And the Moon's with a girdle of pearl;
The volcanoes are dim, and the stars reel and
  swim
  When the whirlwinds my banner unfurl.
From cape to cape, with a bridge-like shape,
  Over a torrent sea,
Sunbeam-proof, I hang like a roof,—
  The mountains its columns be.
The triumphal arch through which I march
  With hurricane, fire, and snow,
When the Powers of the air are chained to my chair,
  Is the million-coloured bow;
The sphere-fire above its soft colours wove,
  While the moist Earth was laughing below.

I am the daughter of Earth and Water,
    And the nursling of the Sky;
I pass through the pores of the ocean and shores:
    I change, but I cannot die.
For after the rain when with never a stain
    The pavilion of Heaven is bare,
And the wind and sunbeams with their convex
    gleams
    Build up the blue dome of air,
I silently laugh at my own cenotaph,
    And out of the caverns of rain,
Like a child from the womb, like a ghost from the
    tomb,
    I arise and unbuild it again.   PERCY B. SHELLEY

THE TROSSACHS AT SUNSET

THE western waves of ebbing day
    Rolled o'er the glen their level way;
Each purple peak, each flinty spire,
Was bathed in floods of living fire.
But not a setting beam could glow
Within the dark ravines below,
Where twined the path in shadow hid,
Round many a rocky pyramid,
Shooting abruptly from the dell
Its thunder-splintered pinnacle;
Round many an insulated mass,
The native bulwarks of the pass,
Huge as the tower which builders vain
Presumptuous piled on Shinar's plain.

The rocky summits, split and rent,
Formed turret, dome, or battlement,
Or seemed fantastically set
With cupola or minaret,
Wild crests as pagod ever decked,
Or mosque of Eastern architect.
Nor were these earth-born castles bare,
Nor lacked they many a banner fair;
For, from their shivered brows displayed,
Far o'er the unfathomable glade,
All twinkling with the dew-drops sheen,
The brier-rose fell in streamers green,
And creeping shrubs, of thousand dyes,
Waved in the west-wind's summer sighs.

SIR WALTER SCOTT
from *The Lady of the Lake*

SONNET

OH! how I love, on a fair summer's eve,
    When streams of light pour down the golden west,
And on the balmy zephyrs tranquil rest
The silver clouds, far—far away to leave
All meaner thoughts, and take a sweet reprieve
    From little cares; to find, with easy quest,
    A fragrant wild, with Nature's beauty drest,
And there into delight my soul deceive.
There warm my breast with patriotic lore,
    Musing on Milton's fate—on Sydney's bier—
Till their stern forms before my mind arise:

Perhaps on wing of Poesy upsoar,
  Full often dropping a delicious tear,
When some melodious sorrow spells mine eyes.
                                        JOHN KEATS

EVENING SONG

SHEPHERDS all, and maidens fair,
  Fold your flocks up, for the air
'Gins to thicken, and the sun
Already his great course hath run.
See the dewdrops how they kiss
Every little flower that is;
Hanging on their velvet heads
Like a rope of crystal beads.
See the heavy clouds low falling,
And bright Hesperus down calling
The dead night from under ground,
At whose rising mists unsound,
Damps, and vapours fly apace,
Hovering o'er the wanton face
Of these pastures, where they come,
Striking dead both bud and bloom;
Therefore from such danger lock
Everyone his lovèd flock,
And let your dogs lie loose without,
Lest the wolf come as a scout
From the mountain, and ere day
Bear a lamb or kid away;
Or the crafty thievish fox
Break upon your simple flocks.

So secure yourselves from these,
Be not too secure in ease;
Let one eye his watches keep,
Whilst the t'other eye doth sleep;
So you shall good shepherds prove,
And for ever hold the love
Of our great god. Sweetest slumbers
And soft silence fall in numbers
On your eyelids; so farewell,
Thus I end my evening's knell.

JOHN FLETCHER
from *The Faithful Shepherdess*

YOUTH AT THE SUMMIT

I GOT up the mountain edge, and from the top saw the world stretcht out—cornlands and forest, the river winding among meadow-flats, and right off, like a hem of the sky, the moving sea, with snatches of foam, and large ships reaching forward, out-bound. And then I thought no more, but my heart leapt to meet the wind, and I ran, and I ran. I felt my legs under me, I felt the wind buffet me, hit me on the cheek; the sun shone, the bees swept past me singing; and I too sang, shouted, World, world, I am coming!

MAURICE HEWLETT
from *Pan and the Young Shepherd*

SUMMER ENDS NOW

SUMMER ends now; now, barbarous in beauty,
   the stooks arise
Around; up above, what wind-walks! what lovely
   behaviour
Of silk-sack clouds! has wilder, wilful-wavier
Meal-drift moulded ever and melted across skies?

GERARD MANLEY HOPKINS
from *Hurrahing in Harvest*

AUTUMN

While Autumn nodding o'er the yellow plain
Comes jovial on.

JAMES THOMSON

AUTUMN

I LOVE the fitful gust that shakes
  The casement all the day,
And from the glossy elm tree takes
  The faded leaves away,
Twirling them by the window pane
With thousand others down the lane.

I love to see the shaking twig
  Dance till the shut of eve,
The sparrow on the cottage rig,
  Whose chirp would make believe
That Spring was just now flirting by
In Summer's lap with flowers to lie.

I love to see the cottage smoke
  Curl upwards through the trees,
The pigeons nestled round the cote
  On November days like these;
The cock upon the dunghill crowing,
The mill sails on the heath a-going.

The feather from the raven's breast
  Falls on the stubble lea,
The acorns near the old crow's nest
  Drop pattering down the tree;
The grunting pigs, that wait for all,
Scramble and hurry where they fall.

                              JOHN CLARE

SIMPLON PASS

THE brook and road
      Were fellow-travellers in this gloomy
   strait,
And with them did we journey several hours
At a slow pace. The immeasurable height
Of woods decaying, never to be decayed,
The stationary blasts of waterfalls,
And in the narrow rent at every turn
Winds thwarting winds, bewildered and forlorn,
The torrents shooting from the clear blue sky,
The rocks that muttered close upon our ears,
Black drizzling crags that spake by the way-side
As if a voice were in them, the sick sight
And giddy prospect of the raving stream,
The unfettered clouds and region of the Heavens,
Tumult and peace, the darkness and the light—
Were all like workings of one mind, the features
Of the same face, blossoms upon one tree;
Characters of the same great Apocalypse,
The types and symbols of Eternity,
Of first, and last, and midst, and without end.

WILLIAM WORDSWORTH
from *The Prelude, Bk. 6*

ROBIN REDBREAST

GOOD-BYE, good-bye to Summer!
      For Summer's nearly done;
The garden smiling faintly,

Cool breezes in the sun;
  Our thrushes now are silent,
  Our swallows flown away,—
But Robin's here, in coat of brown,
  With ruddy breast-knot gay.
Robin, Robin Redbreast,
  O Robin dear!
Robin sings so sweetly,
  In the falling of the year.

Bright yellow, red, and orange,
  The leaves came down in hosts;
The trees are Indian Princes,
  But soon they'll turn to ghosts;
The leathery pears and apples
  Hang russet on the bough;
It's Autumn, Autumn, Autumn late,
  'Twill soon be Winter now.
Robin, Robin Redbreast,
  O Robin dear!
And what will this poor Robin do?
  For pinching days are near.

The fireside for the cricket,
  The wheat-stack for the mouse,
When trembling night-winds whistle,
  And moan all round the house.
The frosty ways like iron,
  The branches plumed with snow,—
Alas, in Winter dead and dark
  Where can poor Robin go?

Robin, Robin Redbreast,
    O Robin dear!
And a crumb of bread for Robin,
    His little heart to cheer!

WILLIAM ALLINGHAM

GIVE ME THE SPLENDID SILENT SUN

GIVE me the splendid silent sun with his beams
    full-dazzling,
Give me juicy autumnal fruit ripe and red from
    the orchard,
Give me a field where the unmowed grass grows,
Give me an arbour, give me the trellised grape,
Give me fresh corn and wheat, give me serene-
    moving animals teaching content,
Give me nights perfectly quiet as on high plateaus
    west of the Mississippi, and I looking up at the
    stars,
Give me odorous at sunrise a garden of beautiful
    flowers where I can walk undisturbed,
Give me for marriage a sweet-breathed woman of
    whom I should never tire,
Give me a perfect child, give me a way aside from
    the noise of the world a rural domestic life,
Give me to warble spontaneous songs recluse by
    myself, for my own ears only,
Give me solitude, give me Nature, give me again,
    O Nature, your primal sanities!

WALT WHITMAN

THE FIRE OF AUTUMN

ONE morning in the hollows of the meadow land below the wood lay a silver mist. The sun sweeping upwards in its curve beat this away towards noon, but it was a sign. The fire of autumn was kindled: already the little notched leaves of the hawthorn were tinged with the rust of decay, already a bramble leaf was turning red: soon the flames would mount the mightier trees and fan their pale heat among the willows and ash trees round the lake, lick among the drooping elms and the lacquered oaks, and sweep in abandonment with yawning fire of colour through the old beech forest.

HENRY WILLIAMSON
from *The Lone Swallows*

HARVEST

WHEN lofty trees I see barren of leaves,
  Which erst from heat did canopy the herd,
And summer's green all girded up in sheaves
Borne on the bier with white and bristly beard.

WILLIAM SHAKESPEARE
from *Sonnet 12*

SNOWDON

WITH forehead bent
    Earthward, as if in opposition set
Against an enemy, I panted up
With eager pace, and no less eager thoughts.
Thus might we wear a midnight hour away,
Ascending at loose distance each from each,
And I, as chanced, the foremost of the band;
When at my feet the ground appeared to
    brighten,
And with a step or two seemed brighter still;
Nor was time given to ask or learn the cause,
For instantly a light upon the turf
Fell like a flash, and lo! as I looked up
The Moon hung naked in a firmament
Of azure without cloud, and at my feet
Rested a silent sea of hoary mist.
A hundred hills their dusky backs upheaved
All over this still ocean; and beyond,
Far, far beyond, the solid vapours stretched,
In headlands, tongues, and promontory shapes,
Into the main Atlantic, that appeared
To dwindle, and give up his majesty,
Usurped upon far as the sight could reach.
Not so the ethereal vault; encroachment none
Was there, nor loss; only the inferior stars
Had disappeared, or shed a fainter light
In the clear presence of the full-orbed Moon,

Who, from her sovereign elevation, gazed
Upon the billowy ocean, as it lay
All meek and silent, save that through a rift—
Not distant from the shore whereon we stood,
A fixed, abysmal, gloomy, breathing-place—
Mounted the roar of waters, torrents, streams
Innumerable, roaring with one voice!
Heard over earth and sea, and, in that hour,
For so it seemed, felt by the starry heavens.

WILLIAM WORDSWORTH
from The Prelude, Bk. 14

ODE TO AUTUMN

SEASON of mists and mellow fruitfulness!
   Close bosom-friend of the maturing sun;
Conspiring with him how to load and bless
  With fruit the vines that round the thatch-eaves
    run;
To bend with apples the mossed cottage-trees,
  And fill all fruit with ripeness to the core:
  To swell the gourd, and plump the hazel shells
  With a sweet kernel; to set budding more,
And still more, later flowers for the bees,
Until they think warm days will never cease,
  For summer has o'er-brimmed their clammy
    cells.

Who hath not seen thee oft amid thy store?
    Sometimes whoever seeks abroad may find
Thee sitting careless on a granary floor,
    Thy hair soft-lifted by the winnowing wind;
Or on a half-reaped furrow sound asleep,
    Drowsed with the fume of poppies, while thy
        hook
        Spares the next swath and all its twinèd
            flowers;
And sometime like a gleaner thou dost keep
    Steady thy laden head across a brook;
    Or by a cider-press, with patient look,
        Thou watchest the last oozings, hours by
            hours.

Where are the songs of Spring? Ay, where are
    they?
    Think not of them, thou hast thy music too,
While barrèd clouds bloom the soft-dying day,
    And touch the stubble-plains with rosy hue;
Then in a wailful choir, the small gnats mourn
    Among the river sallows, borne aloft
        Or sinking as the light wind lives or dies;
And full-grown lambs loud bleat from hilly bourn;
    Hedge-crickets sing; and now with treble soft
    The redbreast whistles from a garden-croft,
        And gathering swallows twitter in the skies.

                                        JOHN KEATS

SWEET MOURNFUL DAYS

SWEET mournful days, charm of the dreaming
 eyes,
Your beauty is dear to me that says farewell!
I love the sumptuous decline of nature's life,
The tents of the forest adorned with purple and
 gold,
And loud with the sound of the faster breath of the
 wind,
A billowy curtain of fog concealing the sky,
And the sun's rare beam, and the early frost,
And the threat of the grey-head winter standing
 off!

MAX EASTMAN
from *Autumn*

A SEASON OF CONTRASTS

AUTUMN is here and it is already late. He has
 painted the hedges russet and gold, scarlet and
black, and a tangle of grey; now he has damp
brown leaves in his hair and frost in his finger-tips.

It is a season of contrasts; at first all is stir and
bustle, the ingathering of man and beast; barn
and rickyard stand filled with golden treasure; at
the farm the sound of threshing; in wood and
copse the squirrels busied 'twixt tree and store-
house, while the ripe nuts fall with thud of thunder
rain. When the harvesting is over, the fruit

gathered, the last rick thatched, there comes a pause. Earth strips off her bright colours and shows a bare and furrowed face; the dead leaves fall gently and sadly through the calm, sweet air; grey mists drape the fields and hedges. The migratory birds have left, save a few late swallows; and as I sit at work in the soft, still rain, I can hear the blackbird's melancholy trill and the thin pipe of the redbreast's winter song—the air is full of the sound of farewell.

MICHAEL FAIRLESS
from *The Roadmender*

THE MOODS OF THE SEA

AT Boscastle the sea is almost always in movement, tossing restlessly, leaping at the rocks, whitening around them, flecked here and there with white, and the whole sea moves, as if the depths under it moved too. Even then where is not wind enough to ridge the water into separate waves, some energy seems to shoulder up through the surface and push for shore. When the wind urges it, it heaves into great billows, that rise up green and tilt over with a little burst of white, and roll one over another towards the shore, and as they come into a space of curdling foam, curdle, and turn to foam, and leap suddenly at the rocks, and hammer at them with a loud voluminous softness, and fall back like a blown cataract, every drop distinct in the sunlight. It is as if a dome of

whiteness sprang into the air and fell over with a
crash of all its architecture of bubbles. Sometimes
two columns of foam meet in the air, and pass
through one another like a ghost through a ghost.
Sometimes a great wave springs higher at the
rocks, seems to take hold there, and then falls
back, broken into spray, while the rock streams
steadily; and then, after a pause, a thin white
smoke-drift, incredibly thin and white, like the
reflection of smoke in a glass, is blown far out from
some corner or crevice in the rock that had sucked
the water deep into it.

ARTHUR SYMONS
from *Cornish Sketches*

THE HAUGHTY THISTLE

THE nodding oxeye bends before the wind,
The woodbine quakes lest boys their flowers
should find,
And prickly dogrose spite of its array
Can't dare the blossom-seeking hand away,
While thistles wear their heavy knobs of bloom
Proud as a war horse wears its haughty plume,
And by the roadside danger's self defy;
On commons where pined sheep and oxen lie
In ruddy pomp and ever thronging mood
It stands and spreads like danger in a wood,
And in the village street where meanest weeds
Can't stand untouch'd to fill their husks with
seeds,

The haughty thistle o'er all danger towers,
In every place the very wasp of flowers.

JOHN CLARE

THE FAWN

WITH sweetest milk and sugar, first
    I, it at mine own fingers nurst;
And as it grew, so every day
It waxed more white and sweet than they
It had so sweet a breath! And oft
I blushed to see its foot more soft
And white, shall I say than my hand?
Nay, any Lady's in the land.

It is a wondrous thing how fleet
'Twas on those little silver feet.
With what a pretty skipping grace,
It oft would challenge me the race;
And when't had left me far away,
'Twould stay, and run again, and stay;
For it was nimbler much than hinds,
And trod as if on the four winds.

I have a garden of my own,
But so with roses overgrown,
And lilies, that you would it guess
To be a little wilderness.
And all the springtime of the year
It lovèd only to be there.

Among the beds of lilies I
Have sought it oft, where it should lie:
Yet could not, till itself should rise,
Find it, although before mine eyes;
For in the flaxen lilies' shade
It like a bank of lilies laid.

Upon the roses it would feed,
Until its lips e'en seemed to bleed;
And then to me 'twould boldly trip,
And print those roses on my lip.

But all its chief delight was still
On roses thus itself to fill;
And its pure virgin limbs to fold
In whitest sheets of lilies cold.
Had it lived long, it would have been
Lilies without, roses within.

ANDREW MARVELL

INVERSNAID

THIS darksome burn, horseback brown,
This rollrock highroad roaring down,
In coop and in comb the fleece of his foam
Flutes and low to the lake falls home.

A windpuff-bonnet of fawn-froth
Turns and twindles over the broth
Of a pool so pitchblack, fell-frowning,
It rounds and rounds Despair to drowning.

Degged with dew, dappled with dew
Are the groins of the braes that the brook treads
   through,
Wiry heathpacks, flitches of fern,
And the beadbonny ash that sits over the burn.

What would the world be, once bereft
Of wet and of wildness? Let them be left,
O let them be left, wildness and wet;
Long live the weeds and the wilderness yet.

GERARD MANLEY HOPKINS

THE STAG

THERE is no more beautiful creature than a stag
in his pride of antler, his coat of ruddy gold,
his grace of form and motion. He seems the natural
owner of the ferny coombes, the oak woods, the
broad slopes of heather. They belong to him,
and he steps upon the sward in lordly mastership.
The land is his, and the hills, the sweet streams
and rocky glens. He is infinitely more natural than
the cattle and sheep that have strayed into his
domains. For some inexplicable reason, although
they too are in reality natural, when he is present
they look as if they had been put there and were
kept there by artificial means. They do not, as
painters say, shade in with the colours and shape
of the landscape. He is as natural as an oak, or
a fern, or a rock itself. He is earth-born—autoch-

thon—and holds possession by descent. Utterly scorning control, the walls and hedges are nothing to him—he roams where he chooses, as fancy leads, and gathers the food that pleases him.

Pillaging the crops and claiming his dues from the orchards and gardens, he exercises his ancient feudal rights, indifferent to the laws of house-people. Disturb him in his wild strong-hold of oak wood or heather, and, as he yields to force, still he stops and looks back proudly. He is slain, but never conquered. He will not cross with the tame park deer; proud as a Spanish noble, he disdains the fallow deer, and breeds only with his own race. But it is chiefly because of his singular adaptation and fitness to the places where he is found that he obtains our sympathy.

The branching antlers accord so well with the deep shadowy boughs and the broad fronds of the brake; the golden red of his coat fits to the fox-glove, the purple heather, and later on to the orange and red of the beech; his easy bounding motion springs from the elastic sward; his limbs climb the steep hill as if it were level; his speed covers the distances, and he goes from place to place as the wind. He not only lives in the wild, wild woods and moors—he grows out of them, as the oak grows from the ground. The noble stag in his pride of antler is lord and monarch of all the creatures left to us in English forests and on English hills.

RICHARD JEFFERIES
from *Red Deer*

PIED BEAUTY

GLORY be to God for dappled things—
  For skies of couple-colour as a brinded cow;
    For rose-moles all in stipple upon trout that
      swim;
Fresh-firecoal chestnut-falls; finches' wings;
  Landscapes plotted and pieced—fold, fallow and
    plough;
    And all trades, their gear and tackle and trim.

All things counter, original, spare, strange;
  Whatever is fickle, freckled (who knows how?)
    With swift, slow; sweet, sour; adazzle, dim;
He fathers-forth whose beauty is past change:
      Praise Him.

                                    GERARD MANLEY HOPKINS

PEACE

THERE came
  A calmness, like the calmness of a grave
Walled safe from all the noisy walks of men
In some green quiet place of peace where
    daisies grow.

                                    LORD LYTTON

UNREPROVÈD PLEASURES FREE

To hear the lark begin his flight,
And singing startle the dull night,
From his watch-tower in the skies,
Till the dappled dawn doth rise;
Then to come in spite of sorrow,
And at my window bid good morrow,
Through the sweet-briar, or the vine,
Or the twisted eglantine.
While the cock with lively din
Scatters the rear of darkness thin,
And to the stack, or the barn-door,
Stoutly struts his dames before,
Oft listening how the hounds and horn
Cheerly rouse the slumbering morn,
From the side of some hoar hill,
Through the high wood echoing shrill:
Some time walking not unseen
By hedge-row elms, on hillocks green,
Right against the eastern gate,
Where the great sun begins his state,
Robed in flames, and amber light,
The clouds in thousand liveries dight.
While the ploughman near at hand
Whistles o'er the furrowed land,
And the milkmaid singeth blithe,
And the mower whets his scythe,
And every shepherd tells his tale
Under the hawthorn in the dale,
Straight mine eye hath caught new pleasures

Whilst the landscape round it measures,
Russet lawns, and fallows grey,
Where the nibbling flocks do stray,
Mountains on whose barren breast
The labouring clouds do often rest:
Meadows trim with daisies pied,
Shallow brooks, and rivers wide.

JOHN MILTON
from *L'Allegro*

THE LITTLE WAVES OF BREFFNY

THE grand road from the mountain goes shining
to the sea,
And there is traffic in it, and many a horse and
cart,
But the little roads of Cloonagh are dearer far to
me,
And the little roads of Cloonagh go rambling
through my heart.

A great storm from the ocean goes shouting o'er
the hill,
And there is glory in it and terror on the wind,
But the haunted air of twilight is very strange and
still,
And the little winds of twilight are dearer to my
mind.

The great waves of the Atlantic sweep storming
    on their way,
      Shining green and silver with the hidden herring
        shoal,
But the Little Waves of Breffny have drenched my
    heart in spray,
      And the Little Waves of Breffny go stumbling
        through my soul.

EVA GORE BOOTH

ODE TO THE WEST WIND

I

O WILD West Wind, thou breath of Autumn's
    being,
Thou, from whose unseen presence the leaves dead
Are driven, like ghosts from an enchanter fleeing,

Yellow, and black, and pale, and hectic red,
Pestilence-stricken multitudes! O thou,
Who chariotest to their dark wintry bed

The wingèd seeds, where they lie cold and low,
Each like a corpse within its grave, until
Thine azure sister of the Spring shall blow

Her clarion o'er the dreaming earth, and fill
(Driving sweet buds like flocks to feed in air)
With living hues and odours plain and hill:

Wild Spirit, which art moving everywhere;
Destroyer and preserver; hear, oh, hear!

II

Thou on whose stream, 'mid the steep sky's com-
    motion,
Loose clouds like earth's decaying leaves are shed,
Shook from the tangled boughs of Heaven and
    Ocean,

Angels of rain and lightning: there are spread
On the blue surface of thine aery surge,
Like the bright hair uplifted from the head

Of some fierce Maenad, even from the dim verge
Of the horizon to the zenith's height,
The locks of the approaching storm. Thou dirge

Of the dying year, to which this closing night
Will be the dome of a vast sepulchre,
Vaulted with all thy congregated might

Of vapours, from whose solid atmosphere
Black rain, and fire, and hail will burst: oh, hear!

III

Thou who didst waken from his summer dreams
The blue Mediterranean, where he lay,
Lulled by the coil of this crystàlline streams,

Beside a pumice isle in Baiæ's bay,
And saw in sleep old palaces and towers
Quivering within the wave's intenser day,

All overgrown with azure moss and flowers
So sweet, the sense faints picturing them! Thou
For whose path the Atlantic's level powers

Cleave themselves into chasms, while far below
The sea-blooms and the oozy woods which wear
The sapless foliage of the ocean, know

Thy voice, and suddenly grow gray with fear,
And tremble and despoil themselves: oh, hear!

IV

If I were a dead leaf thou mightest bear;
If I were a swift cloud to fly with thee;
A wave to pant beneath thy power, and share

The impulse of thy strength, only less free
Than thou, O uncontrollable! If even
I were as in my boyhood, and could be

The comrade of thy wanderings over Heaven,
As then, when to outstrip thy skiey speed
Scarce seemed a vision; I would ne'er have striven

As thus with thee in prayer in my sore need.
Oh, lift me as a wave, a leaf, a cloud!
I fall upon the thorns of life! I bleed!

A heavy weight of hours has chained and bowed
One too like thee: tameless, and swift, and proud.

V

Make me thy lyre, even as the forest is:
What if my leaves are falling like its own!
The tumult of thy mighty harmonies

Will take from both a deep, autumnal tone,
Sweet though in sadness. Be thou, Spirit fierce,
My spirit! Be thou me, impetuous one!

Drive my dead thoughts over the universe
Like withered leaves to quicken a new birth!
And, by the incantation of this verse,

Scatter, as from an unextinguished hearth
Ashes and sparks, my words among mankind!
Be through my lips to unawakened earth

The trumpet of a prophecy! O wind,
If Winter comes, can Spring be far behind?

PERCY B. SHELLEY

MIST

Low-anchored cloud,
Newfoundland air,
Fountain-head and source of rivers,
Dew-cloth, dream-drapery,
And napkin spread by fays;
Drifting meadow of the air,
Where bloom the daisied banks and violets,

And in whose fenny labyrinth
The bittern booms and heron wades;
Spirit of lakes and seas and rivers,
Bears only perfumes and the scent
Of healing herbs to just men's fields.

HENRY DAVID THOREAU

HAY MAKING

UPON the grass no longer hangs the dew;
  Forth hies the mower, with his glittering
  scythe,
In snowy shirt bedight, and all unbraced,
He moves athwart the mead with sidling bend,
And lays the grass in many a swathey line:
In every field, in every lawn and meadow,
The rousing voice of industry is heard;
The haycock rises, and the frequent rake
Sweeps on the fragrant hay in heavy wreaths.
The old and young, the weak and strong, are there,
And, as they can, help on the cheerful work.
The father jeers his awkward half-grown lad,
Who trails his tawdry armful o'er the field,
Nor does he fear the jeering to repay.
The village oracle, and simple maid,
Jest in their turns and raise the ready laugh;
All are companions in the general glee;
Authority, hard-favoured, frowns not there.
Some, more advanced, raise up the lofty rick,
Whilst on its top doth stand the parish toast,
In loose attire, and swelling ruddy cheek.

With taunts and harmless mockery she receives
The tossed-up heaps from fork of simple youth,
Who, staring on her, takes his arm away,
While half the load falls back upon himself.
Loud is her laugh, her voice is heard afar:
The mower busied on the distant lawn,
The carter trudging on his dusty way,
The shrill sound know, their bonnets toss in air,
And roar across the field to catch her notice:
She waves her arm to them, and shakes her head,
And then renews her work with double spirit.
Thus do they jest and laugh away their toil
Till the bright sun, now past his middle course,
Shoots down his fiercest beams which none may
    brave.
The stoutest arm feels listless, and the swart
And brawny-shouldered clown begins to fail,
But to the weary, lo! there comes relief!
A troop of welcome children o'er the lawn
With slow and wary steps approach: some bear
In baskets oaten cakes or barley scones,
And gusty cheese and stoups of milk or whey.
Beneath the branches of a spreading tree,
Or by the shady side of the tall rick,
They spread their homely fare, and seated round,
Taste every pleasure that a feast can give.

                              JOANNA BAILLIE

MELROSE ABBEY

IF thou would'st view fair Melrose aright,
Go visit it by the pale moonlight;
For the gay beams of lightsome day
Gild, but to flout, the ruins grey.
When the broken arches are black in night,
And each shafted oriel glimmers white;
When the cold light's uncertain shower
Streams on the ruined central tower;
When buttress and buttress, alternately,
Seem framed of ebon and ivory;
When silver edges the imagery,
And the scrolls that teach thee to live and die;
When distant Tweed is heard to rave,
And the owlet to hoot o'er the deadman's grave,
Then go—but go alone the while—
Then view St. David's ruined pile;
And, home returning, soothly swear,
Was never scene so sad and fair!

SIR WALTER SCOTT
from *The Lay of the Last Minstrel*

AMONG THE ROCKS

OH, good gigantic smile o' the brown old earth,
This autumn morning! How he sets his
bones
To bask i' the sun, and thrusts out knees and feet
For the ripple to run over in its mirth;

Listening the while, where on the heap of stones
The white breast of the sea-lark twitters sweet.

That is the doctrine, simple, ancient, true;
    Such is life's trial, as old earth smiles and knows.
If you loved only what were worth your love,
Love were clear gain, and wholly well for you:
    Make the low nature better by your throes!
Give earth yourself, go up for gain above.

ROBERT BROWNING

HEAP HIGH THE FARMER'S
WINTRY HOARD!

HEAP high the farmer's wintry hoard!
    Heap high the golden corn!
No richer gift has Autumn poured
    From out her lavish horn!

Let other lands, exulting, glean
    The apple from the pine,
The orange from its glossy green,
    The cluster from the vine;

We better love the hardy gift
    Our rugged vales bestow,
To cheer us when the storm shall drift
    Our harvest-fields with snow.

Through vales of grass and meads of flowers,
    Our ploughs their furrows made,
While on the hills the sun and showers
    Of changeful April played.

We dropped the seed o'er hill and plain,
 Beneath the sun of May,
And frightened from our sprouting grain
 The robber crows away.

All through the long, bright days of June
 Its leaves grew green and fair,
And waved in hot midsummer's noon
 Its soft and yellow hair.

And now, with autumn's moonlit eves,
 Its harvest-time has come,
We pluck away the frosted leaves,
 And bear the treasure home.

There, richer than the fabled gift
 Apollo showered of old,
Fair hands the broken grain shall sift,
 And knead its meal of gold.

JOHN G. WHITTIER
from The Corn-Song

THE WHITE BLACKBIRDS

Among the stripped and sooty twigs of the wild
 cherry tree
Sometimes they flit and swing as though two
 blossoms of the Spring
Had quickened on these bleak October branches
 suddenly.

They are like fairy birds flown down from skies
    which no one knows,
Their pointed yellow bills are bright as April
    daffodils,
Their plumy whiteness heavenly as January snows.

Loveliest guests that choose our garden-plot for
    loitering!
Oh, what a sudden flower of joy is set upon the
    hour
When in their cherry cages two white blackbirds
    sit and swing.

ELEANOR FARJEON

THE PLOUGH

ABOVE yon sombre swell of land
    Thou see'st the dawn's grave orange hue,
With one pale streak like yellow sand,
    And over that a vein of blue.

The air is cold above the woods;
    All silent is the earth and sky,
Except with his own lonely moods
    The blackbird holds a colloquy.

Over the broad hill creeps a beam,
    Like hope that gilds a good man's brow;
And now ascends the nostril-stream
    Of stalwart horses come to plough.

Ye rigid Ploughmen, bear in mind
 Your labour is for future hours:
Advance—spare not—nor look behind—
 Plough deep and straight with all your powers.

RICHARD H. HORNE

THE LOVE-SONG OF THE GREENSHANK

WE were near the nesting-place of three birds, each of them unusual and striking, which were true natives of deer-forest country—the black-throated diver, the greenshank, and the ptarmigan. We would therefore climb the hill behind the eyrie and step out on to rolling moorlands with a hill loch at our feet. It would be here, perhaps, that my companion would have an experience of a fresh and wonderful song—the love-song of the greenshank. In the cloud-flecked sky, so high that he could be seen with difficulty, a small object would madly dart in broad circles, travelling at great speed, and pouring out its song without pause, and without seeming to draw breath, minute after minute for the space of perhaps half an hour. This wild music would be something entirely new to my friend; he would mark a curious spiritual quality in the song, a strange excitement and passion, as though the singer were rising to an ecstasy of joy. Then, the song over and the passion liberated, the singer

would fly gently down to the shore of the loch
and alight quietly beside some sandy bay, there
to gaze pensively across the water.

SETON GORDON
from *Bird Life*

THE OWL

WHEN cats run home and light is come,
    And dew is cold upon the ground,
And the far-off stream is dumb,
    And the whirring sail goes round,
    And the whirring sail goes round;
        Alone and warming his five wits,
        The white owl in the belfry sits.

When merry milkmaids click the latch,
    And rarely smells the new-mown hay,
And the cock hath sung beneath the thatch
    Twice or thrice his roundelay,
    Twice or thrice his roundelay;
        Alone and warming his five wits,
        The white owl in the belfry sits.

ALFRED TENNYSON

THE JOYS OF THE ROAD

Now the joys of the road are chiefly these:
    A crimson touch on the hard-wood trees:

A vagrant's morning wide and blue,
In early fall, when the wind walks, too;

A shadowy highway cool and brown,
Alluring up and enticing down

From rippled water to dappled swamp,
From purple glory to scarlet pomp;

The outward eye, the quiet will,
And the striding heart from hill to hill;

The tempter apple over the fence;
The cobweb bloom on the yellow quince;

The palish asters along the wood,—
A lyric touch of the solitude;

An open hand, an easy shoe,
And a hope to make the day go through,—

Another to sleep with, and a third
To wake me up at the voice of a bird,

The resonant far-listening morn,
And the hoarse whisper of the corn;

The crickets mourning their comrades lost,
In the night's retreat from the gathering frost;

(Or is it their slogan, plaintive and shrill,
As they beat on their corselets, valiant still?)

A hunger fit for the kings of the sea,
And a loaf of bread for Dickon and me;

A thirst like that of the Thirsty Sword,
And a jug of cider on the board;

An idle noon, a bubbling spring,
The sea in the pine-tops murmuring;

A scrap of gossip at the ferry;
A comrade neither glum nor merry,

Asking nothing, revealing naught,
But minting his words from a fund of thought,

A keeper of silence eloquent,
Needy, yet royally well content,

Of the mettled breed, yet abhorring strife,
And full of the mellow juice of life,

A taster of wine, with an eye for a maid,
Never too bold, and never afraid,

Never heart-whole, never heart-sick,
(These are the things I worship in Dick)

No fidget and no reformer, just
A calm observer of ought and must,

A lover of books, but a reader of man,
No cynic and no charlatan,

Who never defers and never demands,
But, smiling, takes the world in his hands,—

Seeing it good as when God first saw
And gave it the weight of His will for law,

And O the joy that is never won,
But follows and follows the journeying sun,

By marsh and tide, by meadow and stream,
A will-o'-the-wind, a light-o'-dream,

Delusion afar, delight anear,
From morrow to morrow, from year to year.

A jack-o'-lantern, a fairy fire,
A dare, a bliss, and a desire!

The racy smell of the forest loam,
When the stealthy, sad-heart leaves go home:

(O leaves, O leaves, I am one with you,
Of the mould and the sun and the wind and the
    dew!)

The broad gold wake of the afternoon;
The silent fleck of the cold new moon;

The sound of the hollow sea's release,
From stormy tumult to starry peace;

With only another league to wend;
And two brown arms at the journey's end!

These are the joys of the open road—
For him who travels without a load.

BLISS CARMAN

SKY AFTER STORM

A SINGLE step, that freed me from the skirts
   Of the blind vapour, opened to my view
Glory beyond all glory ever seen
By waking sense or by the dreaming soul!
The appearance, instantaneously disclosed,
Was of a mighty city—boldly say
A wilderness of building, sinking far
And self-withdrawn into a boundless depth,
Far sinking into splendour—without end!
Fabric it seemed of diamond and of gold,
With alabaster domes, and silver spires,
And blazing terrace upon terrace, high
Uplifted; here, serene pavilions bright,
In avenues disposed; there, towers begirt
With battlements that on their restless fronts
Bore stars—illumination of all gems!
By earthly nature had the effect been wrought
Upon the dark materials of the storm
Now pacified; on them, and on the coves
And mountain-steeps and summits, whereunto
The vapours had receded, taking there
Their station under a cerulean sky.

Oh, 'twas an unimaginable sight!
Clouds, mists, streams, watery rocks and emerald
   turf,
Clouds of all tincture, rocks and sapphire sky,
Confused, commingled, mutually inflamed,
Molten together, and composing thus,
Each lost in each, that marvellous array
Of temple, palace, citadel, and huge
Fantastic pomp of structure without name,
In fleecy folds voluminous, enwrapped.
Right in the midst, where interspace appeared
Of open court, an object like a throne
Under a shining canopy of state
Stood fixed.

WILLIAM WORDSWORTH
from The Excursion, Bk. 2

ODE TO EVENING

IF ought of oaten stop or pastoral song
  May hope, O pensive Eve, to soothe thine ear,
    Like thy own solemn springs,
     Thy springs, and dying gales,

O nymph reserved, while now the bright-haired
   sun
Sits in yon western tent, whose cloudy skirts,
    With brede ethereal wove,
     O'erhang his wavy bed:

Now air is hushed, save where the weak-eyed bat,
With short shrill shriek, flits by on leathern wing,
    Or where the beetle winds

His small but sullen horn,
As oft he rises 'midst the twilight path,
Against the pilgrim born in heedless hum:
    Now teach me, maid composed,
    To breathe some softened strain,
Whose numbers stealing thro' thy darkening vale,
May not unseemly with its stillness suit,
    As, musing slow, I hail
    Thy genial loved return!

For when thy folding-star arising shows
His paly circlet, at his warning lamp
    The fragrant hours, and elves
    Who slept in buds the day,
And many a nymph who wreaths her brows with
    sedge,
And sheds the fresh'ning dew, and lovelier still,
    The pensive pleasures sweet
    Prepare thy shadowy car.

Then let me rove some wild and heathy scene,
Or find some ruin 'midst its dreary dells,
    Whose walls more awful nod
    By thy religious gleams.
Or if chill blust'ring winds, or driving rain,
Prevent my willing feet, be mine the hut,
    That from the mountain's side,
    Views wilds, and swelling floods,
And hamlets brown, and dim-discovered spires,
And hears their simple bell, and marks o'er all
    Thy dewy fingers draw
    The gradual dusky veil.

While Spring shall pour his showers, as oft he wont,
And bathe thy breathing tresses, meekest Eve!
    While Summer loves to sport
    Beneath thy lingering light;
While sallow autumn fills thy lap with leaves;
Or winter, yelling through the troublous air,
    Affrights thy shrinking train
    And rudely rends thy robes:
So long, regardful of thy quiet rule,
Shall fancy, friendship, science, smiling peace,
    Thy gentlest influence own,
    And love thy favourite name!

WILLIAM COLLINS

WINTER

Nor from the perfect circle of the year
Can even Winter's crystal gems be spared.

CHRISTOPHER PEARSE CRANCH

WINTER

THROUGH the hushed air the whitening shower
    descends,
At first thin-wavering; till at last the flakes
Fall broad and wide and fast, dimming the day
With a continual flow. The cherished fields
Put on their winter-robe of purest white.
'Tis brightness all; save where the new snow
    melts
Along the mazy current.

JAMES THOMSON
from *The Seasons*

NOVEMBER I

How clear, how keen, how marvellously bright
    The effluence from yon distant mountain's
    head,
Which, strewn with snow smooth as the sky can
    shed,
Shines like another sun—on mortal sight
Uprisen, as if to check approaching night,
And all her twinkling stars. Who now would tread,
If so he might, yon mountain's glittering head—
Terrestrial—but a surface, by the flight
Of sad mortality's earth-sullying wing,

Unswept, unstained! Nor shall the aërial powers
Dissolve that beauty—destined to endure,
White, radiant, spotless, exquisitely pure,
Through all vicissitudes—till genial spring
Has filled the laughing vales with welcome flowers.

WILLIAM WORDSWORTH

THE SNOWSTORM

ANNOUNCED by all the trumpets of the sky,
  Arrives the snow, and, driving o'er the fields,
Seems nowhere to alight: the whited air
Hides hills and woods, the river, and the heaven,
And veils the farmhouse at the garden's end.
The sled and traveller stopped, the courier's feet
Delayed, all friends shut out, the housemates sit
Around the radiant fireplace, inclosed
In a tumultuous privacy of storm.

Come, see the north wind's masonry.
Out of an unseen quarry evermore
Furnished with tile, the fierce artificer
Curves his white bastions with projected roof
Round every windward stake, or tree, or door.
Speeding, the myriad-handed, his wild work
So fanciful, so savage, naught cares he
For number or proportion. Mockingly
On coop or kennel he hangs Parian wreaths;
A swan-like form invests the hidden thorn;
Fills up the farmer's lane from wall to wall,

Maugre the farmer sighs; and at the gate
A tapering turret overtops the work.
And when his hours are numbered, and the world
Is all his own, retiring, as he were not,
Leaves, when the sun appears, astonished Art
To mimic in slow structures, stone by stone,
Built in an age, the mad wind's night-work,
The frolic architecture of the snow.

RALPH W. EMERSON

FLOWERS IN WINTER

Painted upon a Porte Livre

How strange to greet, this frosty morn,
    In graceful counterfeit of flowers,
These children of the meadows, born
    Of sunshine and of showers!

How well the conscious wood retains
    The pictures of its flower-sown home,—
The lights and shades, the purple stains,
    And golden hues of bloom!

It was a happy thought to bring
    To the dark season's frost and rime
This painted memory of spring,
    This dream of summer-time.

Our hearts are lighter for its sake,
    Our fancy's age renews its youth,
And dim-remembered fictions take
    The guise of present truth.

A wizard of the Merrimack,—
    So old ancestral legends say,—
Could call green leaf and blossom back
    To frosted stem and spray.

The dry logs of the cottage wall,
    Beneath his touch, put out their leaves;
The clay-bound swallow, at his call,
    Played round the icy eaves.

The settler saw his oaken flail
    Take bud, and bloom before his eyes;
From frozen pools he saw the pale
    Sweet summer lilies rise.

To their old homes, by man profaned,
    Came the sad dryads, exiled long,
And through their leafy tongues complained
    Of household use and wrong.

The beechen platter sprouted wild,
    The pipkin wore its old-time green;
The cradle o'er the sleeping child
    Became a leafy screen.

Haply our gentle friend hath met,
    While wandering in her sylvan quest,

Haunting his native woodland yet
    That Druid of the West;—

And, while the dew on leaf and flower
    Glistened in moonlight clear and still,
Learned the dusk wizard's spell of power,
    And caught his trick of skill.

But welcome, be it new or old,
    The gift which makes the day more bright,
And paints, upon the ground of cold
    And darkness, warmth and light!

Without is neither gold nor green;
    Within, for birds, the birch-logs sing;
Yet, summer-like, we sit between
    The autumn and the spring.

The one, with bridal blush of rose,
    And sweetest breath of woodland balm,
And one whose matron lips unclose
    In smiles of saintly calm.

Fill soft and deep, O winter snow!
    The sweet azalia's oaken dells,
And hide the bank where roses blow,
    And swing the azure bells!

O'erlay the amber violet's leaves,
    The purple aster's brookside home,

Guard all the flowers her pencil gives
  A life beyond their bloom.

And she, when spring comes round again,
  By greening slope and singing flood
Shall wander, seeking, not in vain,
  Her darlings of the wood.

JOHN G. WHITTIER

DANCE OF THE WIND

A WHIRL-BLAST from behind the hill
  Rushed o'er the wood with startling sound;
Then—all at once the air was still,
And showers of hailstones pattered round.
Where leafless oaks towered high above,
I sat within an undergrove
Of tallest hollies, tall and green;
A fairer bower was never seen.
From year to year the spacious floor
With withered leaves is covered o'er.
And all the year the bower is green.
But see! where'er the hailstones drop,
The withered leaves all skip and hop,
There's not a breeze—no breath of air—
Yet here, and there, and every where
Along the floor, beneath the shade
By those embowering hollies made,
The leaves in myriads jump and spring,
As if with pipes and music rare

Some Robin Good-fellow were there,
And all those leaves, in festive glee,
Were dancing to the minstrelsy.

WILLIAM WORDSWORTH

WINTER WITH THE GULF STREAM

THE boughs, the boughs are bare enough
But earth has never felt the snow.
Frost-furred our ivies are and rough

With bills of rime the brambles shew.
The hoarse leaves crawl on hissing ground
Because the sighing wind is low.

But if the rain-blasts be unbound
And from dank feathers wring the drops
The clogged brook runs with choking sound

Kneading the mounded mire that stops
His channel under clammy coats
Of foliage fallen in the copse.

A simple passage of weak notes
Is all the winter bird dare try.
The bugle moon by daylight floats

So glassy white about the sky,
So like a berg of hyaline,
And pencilled blue so daintily,

I never saw her so divine.
But through dark branches, rarely drest
In scarves of silky shot and shine,

The webbed and the watery west
Where yonder crimson fireball sits
Looks laid for feasting and for rest.

I see long reefs of violets
In beryl-covered fens so dim,
A gold-water Pactolus frets

Its brindled wharves and yellow brim,
The waxen colours weep and run,
And slendering to his burning rim

Into the flat blue mist the sun
Drops out and all our day is done.

GERARD MANLEY HOPKINS

WINTER

A WIDOW bird sat mourning for her love
    Upon a wintry bough;
The frozen wind crept on above,
    The freezing stream below.

There was no leaf upon the forest bare,
    No flower upon the ground,
And little motion in the air
    Except the mill-wheel's sound.

PERCY B. SHELLEY

ASH BOUGHS

Not of all my eyes see, wandering on the world,
    Is anything a milk to the mind so, so sighs deep
Poetry to it, as a tree whose boughs break in the
    sky.
Say it is ash-boughs: whether on a December day
    and furled
Fast or they in clammyish lashtender combs creep
Apart wide and new-nestle at heaven most high.
They touch heaven, tabour on it; how their talons
    sweep
The smouldering enormous winter welkin! May
Mells blue and snow white through them, a fringe
    and fray
Of greenery: it is old earth's groping towards the
    steep
        Heaven whom she childs us by.

GERARD MANLEY HOPKINS

ODE TO THE NORTH-EAST WIND

WELCOME, wild North-easter!
   Shame it is to see
Odes to every zephyr;
   Ne'er a verse to thee.
Welcome, black North-easter!
   O'er the German foam;
O'er the Danish moorlands,
   From thy frozen home.
Tired we are of summer,
   Tired of gaudy glare,
Showers soft and steaming,
   Hot and breathless air.
Tired of listless dreaming,
   Through the lazy day:
Jovial wind of winter,
   Turn us out to play!
Sweep the golden reed-beds;
   Crisp the lazy dyke;
Hunger into madness
   Every plunging pike.
Fill the lake with wild-fowl;
   Fill the marsh with snipe;
While on dreary moorlands
   Lonely curlew pipe.
Through the black fir-forest
   Thunder harsh and dry,
Shattering down the snow-flakes
   Off the curdled sky.

Hark! The brave North-easter!
  Breast-high lies the scent,
On by holt and headland,
  Over heath and bent.
Chime, ye dappled darlings,
  Through the sleet and snow.
Who can over-ride you?
  Let the horses go!
Chime, ye dappled darlings,
  Down the roaring blast;
You shall see a fox die
  Ere an hour be past.
Go! and rest to-morrow,
  Hunting in your dreams,
While our skates are ringing
  O'er the frozen streams.
Let the luscious South-wind
  Breathe in lovers' sighs
While the lazy gallants
  Bask in ladies' eyes.
What does he but soften
  Heart alike and pen?
'Tis the hard grey weather
  Breeds hard English men.
What's the soft South-wester?
  'Tis the ladies' breeze,
Bringing home their trueloves
  Out of all the seas:
But the black North-easter,
  Through the snow-storm hurled,

Drives our English hearts of oak
  Seaward round the world.
Come, as came our fathers,
  Heralded by thee,
Conquering from the eastward,
  Lords by land and sea.
Come; and strong within us
  Stir the Vikings' blood;
Bracing brain and sinew;
  Blow, thou wind of God!

CHARLES KINGSLEY

WOODS IN WINTER

WHEN winter winds are piercing chill,
  And through the hawthorn blows the gale,
With solemn feet I tread the hill,
  That overbrows the lonely vale.

O'er the bare upland, and away
  Through the long reach of desert woods,
The embracing sunbeams chastely play,
  And gladden these deep solitudes.

Where, twisted round the barren oak,
  The summer vine in beauty clung,
And summer winds the stillness broke,
  The crystal icicle is hung.

Where, from their frozen urns, mute springs
  Pour out the river's gradual tide,
Shrilly the skater's iron rings,
  And voices fill the woodland side.

Alas! how changed from the fair scene,
  When birds sang out their mellow lay,
And winds were soft, and woods were green,
  And the song ceased not with the day!

But still wild music is abroad,
  Pale, desert woods! within your crowd;
And gathering winds, in hoarse accord,
  Amid the vocal reeds pipe loud.

Chill airs and wintry winds! my ear
  Has grown familiar with your song;
I hear it in the opening year;
  I listen, and it cheers me long.

HENRY W. LONGFELLOW

TO A SNOWFLAKE

WHAT heart could have thought you?—
    Past our devisal
(O filigree petal!)
Fashioned so purely,
Fragilely, surely,
From what Paradisal
Imagineless metal,
Too costly for cost?
Who hammered you, wrought you,
From argentine vapour?—
" God was my shaper.
Passing surmisal,
He hammered, He wrought me,

From curled silver vapour,
To lust of his mind:—
Thou couldst not have thought me!
So purely, so palely,
Tinily, surely,
Mightily, frailly,
Insculped and embossed,
With His hammer of wind,
And His graver of frost."

                                        FRANCIS THOMPSON

THE EAGLE

HE clasps the crag with hookèd hands:
  Close to the sun in lonely lands,
Ringed with the azure world, he stands.

The wrinkled sea beneath him crawls;
He watches from his mountain walls,
And like a thunderbolt he falls.

                                        ALFRED TENNYSON

A STORM IN WINTER

THE keener tempests come: and, fuming dun
  From all the livid east or piercing north,
Thick clouds ascend, in whose capacious womb
A vapoury deluge lies, to snow congealed.
Heavy they roll their fleecy world along,
And the sky saddens with the gathered storm.

Through the hushed air the whitening shower
    descends,
At first thin-wavering; till at last the flakes
Fall broad and wide and fast, dimming the day
With a continual flow. The cherished fields
Put on their winter-robe of purest white.
'Tis brightness all; save where the new snow melts
Along the mazy current. Low the woods
Bow their hoar head; and, ere the languid sun
Faint from the west emits his evening ray,
Earth's universal face, deep-hid and chill,
Is one wild dazzling waste, that buries wide
The works of man. Drooping, the labourer-ox
Stands covered o'er with snow, and then demands
The fruit of all his toil. The fowls of heaven,
Tamed by the cruel season, crowd around
The winnowing store, and claim the little boon
Which Providence assigns them. One alone,
The redbreast, sacred to the household gods,
Wisely regardful of the embroiling sky,
In joyless fields and thorny thickets leaves
His shivering mates, and pays to trusted man
His annual visit. Half afraid, he first
Against the window beats; then brisk alights
On the warm hearth; then, hopping o'er the floor,
Eyes all smiling family askance,
And pecks, and starts, and wonders where he is—
Till, more familiar grown, the table-crumbs
Attract his slender feet.

JAMES THOMSON
from *The Seasons*

THE WINTER WALK AT NOON

How soft the music of those village bells
Falling at intervals upon the ear
In cadence sweet, now dying all away,
Now pealing loud again, and louder still,
Clear and sonorous, as the gale comes on! . . .
The night was winter in his roughest mood;
The morning sharp and clear. But now at noon
Upon the southern side of the slant hills,
And where the woods fence off the northern blast,
The season smiles, resigning all its rage,
And has the warmth of May. The vault is blue
Without a cloud, and white without a speck
The dazzling splendour of the scene below.
Again the harmony comes o'er the vale;
And through the trees I view the embattled tower
Whence all the music. I again perceive
The soothing influence of the wafted strains,
And settle in soft musings as I tread
The walk, still verdant, under oaks and elms,
Whose outspread branches overarch the glade.
The roof, though movable through all its length
As the wind sways it, has yet well sufficed,
And, intercepting in their silent fall
The frequent flakes, has kept a path for me.
No noise is here, or none that hinders thought.
The redbreast warbles still, but is content
With slender notes, and more than half suppress'd;
Pleased with his solitude, and flitting light
From spray to spray, where'er he rests he shakes

From many a twig the pendent drops of ice,
That tinkle in the withered leaves below.

WILLIAM COWPER
from The Task

WRITTEN ON THE FIRST OF DECEMBER

THOUGH now no more the musing ear
   Delights to listen to the breeze,
That lingers o'er the green-wood shade
   I love thee, Winter! well.

Sweet are the harmonies of Spring,
Sweet is the Summer's evening gale,
And sweet the Autumnal winds that shake
   The many-coloured grove.

And pleasant to the sobered soul
The silence of the wintry scene,
When Nature shrouds herself, entranced
   In deep tranquillity.

Not undelightful now to roam
The wild heath sparkling on the sight;
Not undelightful now to pace
   The forest's ample rounds.

And see the spangled branches shine;
And mark the moss of many a hue
That varies the old tree's brown bark,
   Or o'er the grey stone spreads.

And see the clustered berries bright
Amid the holly's gay green leaves;
The ivy round the leafless oak
   That clasps its foliage close.

See Virtue diffident of strength
Clings to Religion's former aid;
So by Religion's aim upheld,
   Endures calamity.

Nor void of beauties now the spring,
Whose waters hid from summer-sun
Have soothed the thirsty pilgrim's ear
   With more than melody.

Green moss shines there with ice incased;
The long grass bends its spear-like form:
And lovely is the silvery scene
   When faint the sun-beams smile.

Reflection too may love the hour
When Nature, hid in Winter's grave,
No more expands the bursting bud,
   Or bids the flowret bloom;

For Nature soon in Spring's best charms,
Shall rise revived from Winter's grave,
Expand the bursting bud again,
   And bid the flower re-bloom.

ROBERT SOUTHEY

SNOW IN MENTEITH

ALL the familiar landmarks were obliterated. The Grampians and the Campsies had taken on new shapes. Woods had turned into masses of raw cotton, and trees to pyramids of wool, with diamonds here and there stuck in the fleece. The trunks of beeches stood out black upon the lee, and on the weather side were coated thick with snow as hard as sugar on a cake. The boughs of firs and spruces swayed gently up and down under the weight of snow, which bent them towards the ground.

Birches were covered to their slenderest twigs with icicles. Only the larches, graceful and erect, were red, for on their feathery branches snow could find no resting-place. On the rough bark and knotted trunks of oak trees feathery humps bulged out, through which protruded shoots with sere brown leaves still clinging to them, and on them ruffled birds sat moping, twittering in the cold.

A new and silent world, born in a night, had come into existence, and over it brooded a hush, broken but by the cawing of the crows, which fabulated as they flew, perhaps upon the strangeness of the pervading white.

R. B. CUNNINGHAME GRAHAM
from *Progress*

CHRISTMAS DAY

How will it dawn, the coming Christmas
   Day?
A northern Christmas, such as painters love,
And kinsfolk, shaking hands but once a year,
And dames who tell old legends by the fire?
Red sun, blue sky, white snow, and pearled ice,
Keen ringing air, which sets the blood on fire,
And makes the old man merry with the young,
Through the short sunshine, through the longer
   night?
Or southern Christmas, dark and dank with mist,
And heavy with the scent of steaming leaves,
And rosebuds mouldering on the dripping porch;
One twilight, without rise or set of sun,
Till beetles drone along the hollow lane,
And round the leafless hawthorne, flitting bats
Hawk the pale moths of winter? Welcome then
At best, the flying gleam, the flying shower,
The rain-pools glittering on the long white roads,
And shadows sweeping on from down to down
Before the salt Atlantic gale: yet come
In whatsoever garb, or gay or sad,
Come fair, come foul, 'twill still be Christmas Day.

CHARLES KINGSLEY
from *Christmas Day, 1868*

SONG

If there were dreams to sell,
    What would you buy?
Some cost a passing bell;
    Some a light sigh,
That shakes from Life's fresh crown
Only a rose-leaf down.
If there were dreams to sell,
Merry and sad to tell,
And the crier rang the bell,
    What would you buy?

A cottage lone and still,
    With bowers nigh,
Shadowy, my woes to still,
    Until I die.
Such pearl from Life's fresh crown
Fain would I shake me down.
Were dreams to have at will,
This would best heal my ill,
    This would I buy.

THOMAS LOVELL BEDDOES
from *Dream-Pedlary*

EPILOGUE

With the open air and a leisurely life,
  Homespun, and spaniels, and honey,
An eave-full of swallows, a sun-browned wife
  He's never a thought for money.

T. FARQUHARSON

INDEX OF TITLES

INDEX OF AUTHORS

ACKNOWLEDGMENTS

CORDIAL acknowledgments are here tendered to the following authors, publishers and owners of copyright who have given permission for poems and prose passages to appear in these pages.

MESSRS. J. M. DENT & SONS LTD., THE ROYAL SOCIETY FOR THE PROTECTION OF BIRDS and E. P. DUTTON & CO. INC., for the prose passage *Flowers* from *The Book of a Naturalist* by W. H. Hudson.

MESSRS. ELKIN MATHEWS LTD., for the poem *The Joys of the Road* by Bliss Carman.

MESSRS. JOHN LANE THE BODLEY HEAD LTD., for the prose passage *Youth at the Summit* from *Pan and the Young Shepherd* by Maurice Hewlett.

MR. A. F. TSCHIFFELEY for the prose passage *Snow in Menteith* from *Progress* by R. B. Cunninghame Graham.

MR. SETON GORDON for the passage *The Love-Song of the Greenshank* from his book *Bird Life*.

SIR FRANCIS MEYNELL for the poem *To a Snowflake* by Francis Thompson.